Savings Groups at the Frontier

Praise for this book

'The number of "savings groups" – local savings-and-loan clubs promoted and refined by NGOs and others – is growing fast, and their potential to help millions of poorer people manage their money better is clear. This well-written book skilfully balances the thrill of witnessing an exciting new movement emerge with a sober and carefully documented assessment of the challenges it faces.'

Stuart Rutherford OBE, founder of SafeSave, author of The Poor and their Money

'The Arusha Savings Group Summit spawned this excellent book not just to gather together what we now know about savings groups but also as a manifesto of confidence that savings groups offer a very powerful way for the poor to help themselves and each other.'

Chris Dunford, Director of The Evidence Project at Freedom from Hunger

'Nelson and friends provide a refreshing view of a niche in the microfinance industry where saving, rather than lending, is featured. The savings groups, so ably discussed in this book, are proving to be an inexpensive way of providing financial services to poor people, particularly in rural areas.

'Three features of the book appealed to me: the emphasis on savings as a way of easing poverty; the recognition that informal finance provides valuable lessons for those designing programmes for poor people; and the solid body of knowledge that exists about how to design, promote, and support savings groups.'

Dale W. Adams, Professor Emeritus, The Ohio State University

'Microfinance has for too long been focused on 'microcredit', that is, getting poor people into debt. We are at last realizing that savings must be the starting point for financial inclusion, and saving money, like losing weight, is most easily done in groups. This book shows us what should have been the beginning of microfinance.'

Malcolm Harper, Emeritus Professor of Enterprise Development,
Cranfield University, UK

'For practitioners, facilitators and donors who are already engaged or intend to become engaged with savings groups, the book presents a practical analysis of different implementation methods, monitoring frameworks, costs, sustainability strategies, and the impact of savings groups. This is a useful guide about an approach that is reaching people in more remote and rural areas who have little or no access to financial services.'

Ann J. Miles, Director of Microfinance, The MasterCard Foundation

Savings Groups at the Frontier

Edited by Candace Nelson

PRACTICAL ACTION
Publishing

Practical Action Publishing Ltd
The Schumacher Centre
Bourton on Dunsmore, Rugby,
Warwickshire CV23 9QZ, UK
www.practicalactionpublishing.org

ISBN 978 1 85339 776 9 Hardback
ISBN 978 1 85339 777 6 Paperback
ISBN 978 1 78044 776 6 Library Ebook
ISBN 978 1 78044 777 3 Ebook

Candace Nelson, ed. (2013) *Savings Groups at the Frontier*,
Practical Action Publishing, Rugby, UK.

Since 1974, Practical Action Publishing (formerly Intermediate Technology
Publications and ITDG Publishing) has published and disseminated books
and information in support of international development work throughout
the world. Practical Action Publishing is a trading name of Practical Action
Publishing Ltd (Company Reg. No. 1159018), the wholly owned publishing
company of Practical Action. Practical Action Publishing trades only in
support of its parent charity objectives and any profits are covenanted back
to Practical Action (Charity Reg. No. 247257, Group VAT Registration
No. 880 9924 76).

Cover photo: A woman participates in a savings group in Mali
Credit: Jeffrey Ashe / Oxfam America
Typeset by S.J.I. Services
Printed by Lightning Source in the USA and UK

Contents

Figures, tables and boxes

Figures

Tables

Boxes

Preface

In 2011, CARE celebrated the 20th anniversary of the first Village Savings and Loan Association (VSLA), created in Niger in 1991. Of course back then the women didn't call their programme a Villages Savings and Loan Association; they much more wisely named it *Mata Masu Dubara* (MMD) – 'Women on the Move'. For them, the savings and loan part was less important than the fact that they were taking collective action to improve their lives. I think of those women often, and I know they are proud to see how far the industry they created has come in empowering women, particularly African women. They are all still members of MMD groups, and still teaching other women in Niger the value of group savings and borrowing, just the way they taught CARE.

When this small handful of women started the first VSLA over 20 years ago, they had no idea they were starting a global movement aimed at achieving financial inclusion for some of the poorest people in the world. But that's just what they did, with savings groups now reaching over 6 million people, predominantly in Africa. These women couldn't access financial services that worked for them, so they started something that would.

While Bangladesh is well known as the home of microcredit, Africa is truly the birthplace of the microsavings movement. Savings groups are a uniquely African solution to poverty and financial exclusion. Savings groups have convinced me that the answers to poverty eradication will come not from the developed world, but from the developing countries themselves.

I first met one of the original MMD members in 2009, at the MicroCredit Summit meeting in Nairobi. We had invited her to attend the summit as our guest and share her learning with us. Her story was utterly unique, yet in some ways it is a story I have heard from nearly every VSLA member I have met. She recounted her desperate poverty as a young wife, and how she was forced to marry off her youngest teenage daughters because her family could no longer afford to feed them. Then she joined an MMD group, and started to save just pennies a week. She used some of those savings to feed her family during the lean months, and invested in growing crops and petty trading. As she grew her small business, she increased her weekly savings. At the same time, she got involved in her village council, and then the district council. And something else started happening; the MMD groups in her community began to network with each other, identifying women in the groups to stand for election in local government to represent their interests. Eventually, one of her fellow MMD members was elected to parliament. She also had the opportunity to speak to parliament about women's issues in her community. And now she was travelling to Kenya to share the story of how MMD had empowered so many women in Niger to change their own lives, their communities, and even their country. By whatever name – Village Savings and Loans, Saving for Change, Saving and Internal Lending Communities – these groups of women, and increasingly men, are taking charge of their lives by using their own resources more effectively.

Recently I met a VSLA member who, through her group, had opened a savings account at Barclays Bank in Uganda. She proudly showed me her Barclays ID card, which included her picture, and told me it was the first form of identification she had ever had. When we talk about the type of women who join VSLA groups, we often call them financially excluded. But this was a reminder to me that financial exclusion is often accompanied by so many other forms of exclusion: from national support programmes, from educational opportunities, from markets and from jobs. For these women, being financially included is the beginning of a process of active participation in their national economy, and truly feeling they are recognized and worthy citizens.

A growing question for the savings group movement is, 'what next?' We are increasingly confident that the basic savings group methodology has significant impact for the poorest households, and we are developing more efficient methods of replication at scale. So what's the next frontier for savings groups? I think the answer comes from the members themselves. As I look across the 21 countries where CARE implements VSLA programmes, I see three major trends: greater access to formal financial services, greater access to markets, and greater access to sociopolitical spaces.

For savings group practitioners, the challenge is how we support our members and facilitate their movement into these new spaces. No person or household stays stagnant. For VSLA members something that once seemed impossible, like running for local election or becoming a tea trader instead of a tea picker, are now realities. Of course with new possibilities come new risks, but I think savings groups give their members the solid financial and social foundation to mitigate these risks and allow them to seize opportunities.

Savings Groups at the Frontier is an excellent resource for those who want to explore where savings groups come from, and where the movement is going. This book, written by leaders in the field, will provide the basis for how the movement evolves over the next decade. No one can predict exactly where it is going, but I think we are all convinced that it will be an exciting revolution, and one that continues to be led by the women and men who are members of the savings groups. In the end, they will decide which innovations and evolutions are most valuable, and they will run with them.

Lauren Hendricks
Executive Director, Access Africa
CARE USA

Acknowledgements

A proper acknowledgement of those who have contributed to this book must start with the Arusha Savings Group Summit. In October 2011, 250 delegates from 46 countries gathered to share, question, and celebrate the experiences of an emerging movement, a movement comprising thousands of savings groups around the world that offer basic financial services to those who were previously financially excluded. This book is an outcome of that meeting. Its chapters build on the shared knowledge and collective experience of a wide range of practitioners, researchers, and donors, extending the discussions initiated at the Summit. The SEEP Network and its Savings-Led Financial Services Working Group (SLWG) are very grateful to the Bill & Melinda Gates Foundation and The MasterCard Foundation, whose support made both the first global gathering of savings group advocates and this book possible.

In keeping with the highly participatory nature of the summit, the SEEP Network facilitated an online global feedback process on the book's content as its chapters were outlined and drafted. After posting chapter drafts on savings-revolution.org, the authors received and responded to comments from dozens of people spread across North America, Africa, and Asia. Contributors are noted within each chapter. The authors, all recognized leaders in savings-led microfinance, committed themselves to spend the extra time that this feedback process requires, and for that, I express my sincerest appreciation.

From conception to completion, both the Summit and this book are the result of tireless support and participation from the SLWG. This group of dedicated professionals has answered every request for conference calls, advice, documentation, reviews, and contributions, both financial and intellectual. In decades of development work, I have never encountered a group so committed to its vision; it is my privilege to coordinate their efforts.

At the SEEP Network, Nisha Singh has been a champion of the book, supporting our efforts at every turn. Katherine Oglietti has provided invaluable technical and editorial support. Like most things SEEP, this book benefits from a shared commitment to share what we know and ask frank questions about that which we still have to learn.

Candace Nelson
Editor and SLWG Co-Facilitator

Acronyms and abbreviations

AFI   Alliance for Financial Inclusion
CBO   community-based organization
CBT   community-based trainer
CPM   cost per member
CVECA   *Caisses Villageoises D'épargne et de Crédit Autogérées*
             (self-reliant village savings and credit bank)
FA   facilitating agency
FBO   faith-based organization
FFH   Freedom from Hunger
FFS   fee-for-service
FSD   financial sector deepening
IGA   income-generating activity
INGO   international non-governmental organization
IRC   International Rescue Committee
MFI   microfinance institution
MIS   management information system
MMD   Mata Masu Dubara
NBFI   non-bank financial institution
NGO   non-governmental organization
OVC   orphans and vulnerable children
ROSCA   Rotating Savings and Credit Association
SACCO   Savings and Credit Cooperative
SfC   Saving for Change (Oxfam America, Freedom from Hunger and the
             Stromme Foundation programme)
SG   savings group
SHG   self-help group
SILC   Savings and Internal Lending Community (CRS programme)
TOC   theory of change
VSLA   Village Savings and Loan Association (CARE programme)

Introduction

Jeffrey Ashe and Candace Nelson

Twenty years ago, an experiment began in a handful of villages in Niger that has evolved into a powerful approach to improve financial services for the poor: savings groups (SGs), entities that reach those rarely served by financial institutions. At weekly meetings, SG members deposit savings and take out loans, and in the process build commitment, discipline, and mutual assistance. The outcome is empowered groups, made up mostly of women, who manage themselves as tiny financial institutions.

Membership in a savings group enables poor women and men to save and access small loans easily for investment, consumption, health care, and education. When they need cash, members turn to their savings group instead of selling an animal, borrowing from family or money-lenders, selling crops at a steep discount, or simply doing without the money they need. Five, 10, 20, 50, or 100 dollars can make a big difference when money is scarce and income from the harvest is months away. When asked why members like their saving groups, the most common response is: 'Life is much less stressful now.' Savings groups give many people their first experience of accessing a convenient, flexible, affordable financial service that is designed to facilitate frequent, small transactions.

There are savings groups today in 60 countries with more than 6 million members.[1] Most groups are in Africa, but the number in Asia and Latin America is rapidly increasing.[2] Making financial services available to rural communities heretofore unserved or underserved, savings groups are increasing financial inclusion at a fraction of the per-client cost typical of formal financial institutions.

The Arusha Savings Group Summit and *Savings Groups at the Frontier*

This book is both an outcome and a follow-up to the Arusha Savings Group Summit. In early October 2011, over 250 practitioners from 46 countries gathered at the Arusha International Conference Centre in Tanzania.[3] Although most of the delegates came from Africa, some travelled from as far as Cambodia, Azerbaijan, India, Guatemala, and El Salvador. For two and a half days the delegates participated in debates, discussions, and world cafes. They listened attentively as keynote speaker Stuart Rutherford explained how the poor use multiple financial instruments to manage their financial needs, and then tried to convince him that their savings groups were an appropriate tool to facilitate the types of transactions he described. Mobilizing savings groups across the globe, delegates shared their experiences around core themes: how small groups of villagers save money and lend to each other, how their organizations facilitate the formation of these groups, and the difference that participation in savings groups makes for their members.

Although the summit was a meeting of like minds where SG promoters, seasoned veterans of microfinance, and newcomers gathered to celebrate the promise of an emerging movement, the chapters herein reflect an effort to capture the current state of practice with respect to savings groups. In addition, the book focuses on the 'frontier issues' that define the challenges and the future direction of this fast-growing movement. It is the result of collective input from Summit delegates, whose comments and experiences have been incorporated into the chapters that follow.

This introduction provides an overview of the book's themes, in order of the chapters herein. It explores how savings groups work, whom they serve, and how they fit into the financial landscape. It also synthesizes how the basic principles of the SG model translate into operations, and what issues shape the model's future. The introduction concludes with a summary of options for taking savings groups to scale.

The evolution of the savings group model

There are now an estimated 312,000 savings groups worldwide,[4] but every movement has a starting point. The first savings groups were designed 20 years ago in Niger by Moira Eknes, a Norwegian CARE volunteer who sought a solution to women's limited control over their finances. That solution emerged as an improvement on the only financial management mechanism available to most women: the rotating savings and credit association, or ROSCA.[5] Common throughout the developing world, a ROSCA is a small group whose members contribute a fixed amount of money at agreed-upon intervals. The amount collected at each meeting is paid to each member in turn, until all have received the payout.

That ROSCAs have spread organically from village to village long before roads and mass communication, and certainly before NGOs, is a clear sign of their usefulness. However, a ROSCA's simplicity is counterbalanced by risk and lack of flexibility:

- All ROSCA members receive the same amount of money in a predetermined order. Each must wait her turn, regardless of need.[6] There is no mechanism for members to access funds if they all need them at the same time (e.g. to purchase seeds or pay school fees).
- There is no flexibility to contribute more or less than the agreed amount.
- The fund does not grow in value.

- Those who are last in line risk not receiving their payout if the group disbands. Once a member has already received her money, she may be less likely to continue paying, especially if she falls on hard times.

The savings group model that CARE designed and named the Village Savings and Loan Association (VSLA) addresses each of these limitations. Instead of giving the collected funds to one member at a time, members deposit their savings into a group fund from which they can borrow as needed. From these aggregated savings, loans are provided and repaid with interest. At the end of the cycle (usually eight to 12 months), the entire fund is distributed according to the amount each member saved. Members typically earn a return of 20–40 per cent on their savings from the interest paid on loans (and sometimes other fees or earnings).

To ensure transparency and minimize risk, transactions take place in the presence of all the members. Group funds and records are stored in a box with locks requiring one or more 'key keepers' to open. Officers are elected specifically to handle money and record payments. Members report that they trust the group because they see everything that happens to their money.

Minimal risk, maximum transparency, a profitable structure for saving, access to small loans, and an annual lump sum of capital are the hallmarks of the savings group methodology.[7]

While most savings group initiatives follow these basic principles, over time, adaptations have been made. For example, the risk in providing matching funds to groups as an incentive to save has been widely acknowledged. In Zimbabwe, CARE initially matched member savings, and eventually almost all of these groups disbanded because their motivation was to get the match rather than to undertake the disciplined work of saving and building the group's fund (Fowler and Panetta, 2010). Other adaptations tend to increase flexibility by allowing members to save variable amounts, to simplify recordkeeping and enhance self-management, or to encourage volunteers to train groups. For example, many groups have abandoned ledgers for records kept in individual passbooks. In West Africa, Saving for Change developed an oral recordkeeping system in areas of low literacy, dispensing with written records altogether. Adaptation is a dynamic part of the SG story; many of the adaptations we know about are discussed in these chapters. Future adaptations driven by technology or evolving contextual factors may not yet be known, but hold our attention as we witness how SGs manage themselves.

The early VSLAs in Niger have evolved into a growing family of savings group initiatives, including those carried out by Oxfam America/Freedom from Hunger/Stromme Foundation (Saving for Change), Catholic Relief Services (Savings and Internal Lending Communities), The Aga Khan Foundation (Community-based Savings Groups), Pact (WORTH), Plan International, World Vision, Hope International, and the International Rescue Committee, among others. Local NGOs that have built strong SG programmes include Dutabarane (Burundi), CREAM (Uganda), and Ophavela (Mozambique).

Throughout this book, these organizations are referred to as facilitating agencies. They report SG performance data to a global database known as the SAVIX, which enables trend analysis and comparison across regions and programmes. This database is the work of VSL Associates and Hugh Allen, who has had a central role in systematizing and disseminating the SG model since he saw the first groups in Niger.[8]

Savings groups today: how they fit into the financial landscape

Savings groups can be better understood when they are considered as part of a larger landscape of financial services, spanning traditional forms of saving to formal sector banks, MFIs, and credit unions. A comparison with these services highlights how SGs serve a difficult-to-reach group with services especially tailored to their needs.

Traditional savings

The rural poor save money in various ways. Saving at home 'under the mattress' is the most common and most accessible method, which also makes the savings accumulated in this way the most vulnerable to daily spending pressures. Poor women and men invest in gold, silver, and animals to sell at a time of need; but asset values vary with market demand, and one cannot sell half a goat. 'Money guards' store money that would be tempting to spend if kept at home, but they are not always reliable. Savings group members often admit that they are not able to save enough by relying on these means. In savings groups, they develop the discipline to save, encouraged by the commitment of peers, and the opportunity to both put money out of reach, and access small sums as needed.

ASCAs

An Accumulating Savings and Credit Association (ASCA) addresses some of the limitations of ROSCAs presented above. Unlike ROSCAs, ASCA members' savings are pooled for the purpose of lending, and members borrow as needed. ASCAs are well known in some African countries, but are not as common as ROSCAs are across the continent. At least two versions of ASCAs have been promoted by external entities: the savings group and self-help group. While both are essentially ASCAs, a savings group is 'time-bound'. At the end of a predetermined period, the fund is distributed and the group starts a new cycle. The end-of-cycle 'share-out' effectively distributes the group's assets; members receive a lump sum enabling them to purchase non-productive assets or high-price items that are difficult to save for. The share-out also serves as an 'action-audit', builds trust, simplifies accounting, and enables members to leave or new ones to join.

Self-help groups

Self-help groups (SHGs) emerged in India a few years before CARE developed its VSLA model in Niger. Like savings group members, SHG members contribute their savings to a central fund, borrow from the fund, and pay interest on their loans. Unlike savings groups, SHGs are not time-bound; the group's fund continues to grow over time. The major difference between the two models is that most self-help groups also receive loans from banks. Because India has banks in most village clusters, linking them to rural groups is simpler than it is elsewhere in the developing world. Some loans to groups are guaranteed through the Self-Help Group/Bank Linkage programme of the National Bank for Agriculture and Rural Development (NABARD) (Harper, 2002).

The genius of the SHG/Bank Linkage programme is its decentralization. Thousands of NGOs (and some banks) train groups, and thousands of banks or MFIs make loans to them. The NGOs do what they do best – outreach, training, and support – and the banks do what they do best: issuing and managing loans. The number of members of self-help groups linked to banks is a staggering 59.6 million, with 4.58 million groups in India alone (Srinivasan, 2010). Given that approximately 25 per cent of SHGs are not linked to banks, the total number of SHG members is considerably larger. The NABARD SHG programme is one of the largest microfinance initiatives in the world.

Microfinance institutions (MFIs)

The 2010 State of the MicroCredit Campaign Report indicates that worldwide, there are more than 200 million outstanding loans to microfinance clients.[9] Loans from MFIs are most appropriate for the 'entrepreneurial poor': those with a business that can effectively use credit to finance growth, and who can repay loans with future earnings. Most clients are concentrated in urban and peri-urban areas, except in densely populated Bangladesh, India, and Indonesia. Some MFIs and other financial institutions are diversifying products and services to include a range of credit, savings, and insurance products that savings groups would be hard-pressed to provide. With that said, formal financial institutions, including MFIs, find it difficult to serve the typical SG member profitably. The costs of staff, transport, and infrastructure cannot be supported by the small transactions typically made by the rural poor. At the same time, given the choice, it is not uncommon for people to leave MFIs to join a savings group; members can readily explain their reasons:

- SG transactions occur in the village. There is no need to travel to a bank branch.
- Profits return to the group and build the savings of each member.
- There is little risk of losing an asset because SGs do not require collateral.
- SGs offer more flexibility in case of a late payment.
- Little documentation is required. Loans are discussed and approved by members during the group meeting.[10]

However, over time, a natural segmentation of the market has begun to occur, with smaller transactions being accessed through savings groups and larger loans being provided by MFIs. This segmentation reflects the expertise and financial capacity of each entity. Members can choose the option that best fits their needs.

Credit unions

Credit unions, known by various names around the world, are member-owned, not-for-profit financial cooperatives that provide savings, credit, and other financial services to their members. According to the latest report from the World Council on Credit Unions (WOCCU), there are close to 200 million credit union members in 100 countries (Statistical Report, 2010).[11] Credit union membership is based on a common bond formed by linkage to a specific community, organization, religion, or place of employment. Members benefit from higher returns on savings, lower rates on loans, and fewer fees on average than at commercial financial institutions. Although savings groups can be described as 'mini-credit unions' since they mobilize member savings, loan them out to members, and pay dividends, credit unions are typically larger organizations, and attract people who can afford the required membership fees and initial share purchase.

Clearly, savings groups are a valuable addition to the financial services landscape, because they offer access to a population that most other providers cannot reach. As time-bound ASCAs, SGs improve upon ROSCAs and indigenous non-distributing ASCAs, offering the lump-sum appeal of a ROSCA with the ongoing access to small loans of the ASCA. Furthermore, they are challenging some of the axioms of microfinance – that 'the poor cannot save'. Clearly they can, and savings groups are demonstrating that the pooled savings of 20–30 people can satisfy most smaller financial needs of the poor when they have access to an appropriately designed structure to intermediate their funds. With savings-based alternatives working so well, the notion of going into debt as a primary strategy to mitigate poverty seems almost quixotic.

In the financial landscape, savings groups fill the gap between informal mechanisms and brick-and-mortar institutions; their services are organized, safe, and transparent, yet do not require the infrastructure or costs of formal finance. SGs therefore challenge the assumption that specialized financial institutions are the best option for delivering microfinance. Competent NGOs working in such diverse fields as health, agriculture, and literacy, to name a few, are successfully training savings groups around the world. Furthermore, the SG model calls for groups to develop the capacity to manage themselves within nine to 18 months. Self-management is not a new concept to group members; the SG model is based on traditions of mutual accountability that have underpinned village culture for centuries. Savings groups therefore represent a path to financial inclusion that does not rely on the involvement of financial institutions.

An overview of the contents

In the industry dialogue and global estimates of financial inclusion, most savings group practitioners, not surprisingly, believe that SG members should be counted as financially included. In Chapter 1, 'Savings groups and financial inclusion', Joanna Ledgerwood and Alyssa Jethani posit a financial market systems approach as the conceptual foundation for this argument. They place savings groups in the core of the financial market system where supply and demand meet (along with all other providers, of course). In addition to providing basic financial services, savings groups build members' financial capability, a key piece in the financial inclusion puzzle.

To further cement SGs' role in financial inclusion, the authors acknowledge that savings groups can be effectively linked to formal financial service providers. While practitioners long have debated the need for and merits of linking SGs to the formal financial system, enterprising individual members have found their own way to the bank and FAs, notably CARE, are committed to developing these linkages for the groups. Can groups link to formal finance in a way that benefits both the savings groups and the financial institution? In this chapter, Ledgerwood and Jethani recount the most recent experience with emergent linkage programmes and share guidelines for this endeavour.

In Chapter 2, 'Savings group outreach and membership', Susan Johnson and Silvia Storchi review available data to construct a profile of SG members, and confirm that they are largely rural, female, and poorer than the typical MFI client. SGs have also been successfully introduced to marginalized groups, and the authors review the modifications made to accommodate them. They link features of the SG methodology to the member profile, and suggest ways in which gender, religion, and other factors may affect SG operations.

In Chapter 3, 'Approaches to group formation', Paul Rippey and Hugh Allen tackle the big issues associated with launching savings groups, including costs, institutional roles, and long-term sustainability. Most facilitating agencies make efforts to drive down costs by limiting how much time their field staff spend on training and supporting individual SGs. After a relatively short period of time (9–18 months), groups can survive without ongoing outside support. Groups not only survive, but also replicate, meaning that an investment in forming one group can yield two or three more. However, independence or 'graduation' does not mean that groups never ask for help. As they evolve, groups are likely to encounter situations for which they require advice. In some areas, SGs commonly request help to resolve conflicts or calculate the share-out amounts (Digital Divide Data, 2011), and interestingly, the fee-for-service training models detailed in this chapter accommodate their needs for this occasional assistance. While there is little doubt that replication does occur, many questions remain about the process and the quality of groups thus created. Which aspects of the model get replicated, and which ones are left behind? Are any of the key principles put in place to guarantee transparency and trust compromised in replicated groups that do not receive formal training?

In Chapter 4, Kim Wilson puts a human face on 'Thrift-Led development'. First and foremost, the development that women experience is often personal. It is a mixture of pride in their accomplishment, relief that they no longer suffer the humiliation of begging from family and friends, and solidarity with their SGs as they fight the good fight, again and again, on behalf of fellow members – whether to stop domestic violence or petition local authorities to intervene against injustice. The importance of the social capital that members gain cannot be overstated.

Development can be further defined by the many additional services for which SGs serve as a platform. As well-organized institutions in rural communities, savings groups are natural vehicles for other development initiatives ranging from agricultural production and crop marketing to education in business skills, literacy, and health. Yet adding services to SGs is not straightforward. One must ask whether the 'add-ons' are driven by supply or demand and examine the incentives. Additional costs, ongoing dependency on external service providers, diversion of group funds to the 'extra' services, and spreading group resources (for example, members' time, energy, focus, and funds) too thinly are risks that practitioners must consider. NGOs face the difficult choice between strengthening existing groups with additional programming or spending their scarce resources on creating new ones.

The benefits that SGs create are evident – from members' testimony, their decisions to leave MFIs, and the expressions of gratitude from local government. In Kenya, for example, SGs have reportedly 'solved the school fee problem'.[12] In Chapter 5, 'Impact of group participation', Megan Gash synthesizes what the research on impact reveals, and categorizes the various benefits as having a high, medium, or low chance of occurrence. Not surprisingly, solidarity falls in the 'high' category, along with important financial benefits such as asset accumulation and consumption smoothing.

Finally, a host of sophisticated tools have been brought to bear on the job of tracking and managing SG performance. In Chapter 6, 'Performance monitoring', David Panetta reviews the management information systems that focus on the financial performance of savings groups and the efficiency of the agencies that promote them. For the industry, the SAVIX collects and validates financial and operational data from over 80,000 savings groups in all regions of the developing world. In addition, individual facilitating agencies use a variety of tools from GIS mapping to poverty indexes.

These issues – cost, inputs, replication, group sustainability, integration of financial and non-financial services, linkages to the formal system, and performance – will shape the evolution of savings groups. Not surprisingly, these concerns mirror the preoccupations of the pioneers of microcredit, and in our excitement about savings groups, we should remember that microfinance practitioners have visited these issues before. The main difference now is that these topics are being addressed, not from the perspective of a financial institution, but in support of members and savers who are managing their own financial services.

A vision for the future

In his keynote address at the Arusha Savings Group Summit, Stuart Rutherford said that the ultimate test of success for savings groups is whether the savings group methodology will become as embedded into the fabric of village money management as ROSCAS are today. There are early signs. In Mali, savings groups are springing up spontaneously in those between-the-village spaces where the Saving for Change programme has not yet reached. In Kenya, ROSCAS are reportedly transforming into savings groups. SG members are returning to their birth villages to start savings groups. One delegate at the Arusha Savings Group Summit, for example, was a Ugandan banker who took leave from his job to organize savings groups in his village (see Chapter 4). Some women are making a business out of training groups. Modern technology – facilitating low-cost communication and increased mobility – will foster the spread of these 'improved ROSCAS', speeding their transformation into tradition.

We see several pathways to realize the vision that Stuart Rutherford articulated. First, SG facilitating agencies will continue to build the nascent movement to promote savings groups. Although SG facilitating agencies have trained groups with over six million members, the potential demand for savings groups in Africa alone could easily exceed 80 million.[13] International, national, and local NGOs are now working in concert to cover more territory and meet this demand, but they require resources. The current cost of training and supporting a group of 20 villagers until it can function on its own is about $500 (estimating costs at $25 per member).[14] An investment of one million dollars would bring savings groups to 40,000 villagers, the majority of whom would take loans averaging $39 and earn 30 per cent on their savings.[15] Compared to the costs of building MFIs and financing their commercial transformation, savings groups offer an inexpensive path to financial inclusion.

Second, the myriad institutions that work in villages promoting literacy, health, agriculture, reforestation, business, water, sanitation, and appropriate technology could also greatly expand the number of savings groups. As a result, many of these community improvement efforts need an organized group as their starting point. Savings groups make sense for integration with these programmes because their financial foundation builds cohesive groups that have the resources to support community development activities.

Third, practitioners can make the spread of savings groups a business proposition that pays its own way. Increasingly, new SGs are paying trainers for their services. We can see a technology-enabled future, in which curricula for training groups are disseminated via the internet, and recordkeeping and MIS data are collected electronically and reviewed online. Socially responsible business managers would have to determine how to make the promotion of SGs profitable while giving poor villagers access to affordable services.

In all likelihood, the spread of savings groups will occur through all these means – programme expansion, organic replication, the adoption of SGs by non-financial NGOs, and by social entrepreneurs. If the model is kept simple, savings groups could become fully integrated into rural, and perhaps, urban culture.

Conclusion

The development of a simple, scalable, low-cost, robust, and self-replicating solution to mitigate some of the worst effects of poverty is critical. Considering the urgency of the need and the paucity of resources, savings groups are, at the very least, a useful starting point. The goal is to create a highly cost-effective and replicable model recognizing the centrality of villagers, especially women, in an increasingly resource-constrained world. To achieve this goal, advocates of savings groups must:

- expand the number of groups and involve new partners;
- reduce costs without sacrificing the overall objective of promulgating autonomous, quality financial service providers for poor women and men;
- learn from each other to document breakthrough experiences among savings group practitioners that point the way to uniquely useful and cost-effective interventions;
- explore the use of technology to manage group funds, link groups to financial institutions, and lower the costs of training and support; and
- communicate the savings group story through publications, videos, conferences, and advocacy. Massive replication calls for widespread awareness and financial support from the full range of donors, as well as the private sector, assuming a business case can be made for supporting the savings movement.

Experience to date demonstrates that savings groups offer a path to financial inclusion for the poor. They start with saving and lending, and in the process, build social and economic capital, often setting the stage for a more ambitious development agenda. Savings groups have been the starting point for increased financial capability, community development efforts, linkages with formal finance, and new opportunities for the traditionally marginalized. Empowered groups are already starting to demand services from local government, and we expect this bottom-up advocacy to expand as savings groups do. As communities and local institutions increasingly take the lead, our task is to help them spread the impact of this promising methodology.

Notes

1. These figures refer to savings groups only; they do not include self-help groups in India.

2. As of May 2012 there were 6,238,571 SG members: 5,633,229 in Africa, 468,366 in Asia, and 136,976, in Latin America. This information was compiled from a working document at VSL Associates.
3. The costs of the Arusha Savings Group Summit were underwritten principally by the Bill & Melinda Gates Foundation and The Master Card Foundation. Others funders include the SEEP Network and the Financial Sector Deepening programmes in Kenya and Tanzania.
4. Based on an estimated average group size of 20, the total number of SGs is 312,000. This information was compiled from a working document at VSL Associates.
5. ROSCAs in Africa have many names: tontine, stokvel, merry-go-round, etc. What is described here is the simplest and most common form of ROSCA.
6. Some ROSCAs permit a member to receive her payout earlier by paying a premium determined by bidding at each meeting.
7. For a detailed description of all elements of the SG methodology, see Allen and Panetta (2010).
8. More information on the SAVIX can be found at: www.thesavix.org, and is discussed in detail in Chapter 6: 'Performance Measurement'.
9. According to the State of the MicroCredit Campaign, as of 31 December 2010 there were 205,314,502 MFI clients.
10. Information from field notes from Saving for Change, Cambodia, in March 2012. Jeffrey Ashe, Director of Community Finance, Oxfam America.
11. According to the World Council of Credit Unions as of December 2010, there were 53,000 credit unions with 188 million members in 100 countries. Available from: www.woccu.org/memberserv/intlcusystem [accessed 6 June 2012].
12. Allan Odera (2012), Program Manager, CARE COSALO II, Kenya. Personal conversation with Candace Nelson.
13. Mali, which has a population of 14 million, has nearly 600,000 SG members. Practitioners estimate that this number could be doubled at a minimum. An assumption that nine per cent of the population of Africa would be interested in joining SGs works out to at least 80 million potential members.
14. Significant variation in cost per member is the result of many factors. See Chapter 3 for a discussion on this indicator.
15. The SAVIX provides average loan size by facilitating agency as follows: Aga Khan Foundation ($59), CARE ($31), CRS ($38.40), Oxfam ($22.20), Plan International ($44.80). Available from: www.thesavix.org.

References

Allen, H. and Panetta, D. (2010) *Savings Groups: What are They?* The SEEP Network Savings-Led Financial Services Working Group, Washington, D.C. Available from: <www.seepnetwork.org/filebin/pdf/resources/Savings_FINAL_web.pdf>

Digital Divide Data (2011) 'Results of study of post-project replication of groups in COSALO I'. Available from: <www.fsdkenya.org/pdf_documents/12-01-20_COSALO_I_short_study.pdf>

Fowler, B. and Panetta, D. (2010) 'Beyond financial services: Improving access to basic financial services and agricultural input and output markets by smallholder farmers in Zimbabwe', Aga Khan Foundation. Available from: <www.akdn.org/publications/beyond_financial_services_access_by_smallholder_farmers_zimbabwe.pdf>.

Harper, M. (2002) *Promotion of Self Help Groups under the SHG Bank Linkage Programme in India*, NABARD, Mumbai. Available from: <www.nabard.org/pdf/publications/sudy_reports/malcolmharper.pdf>

Srinivasan, N. (2010) *Microfinance India: State of the Sector Report 2010*, Sage Publications India and ACCESS Development Services, New Delhi. Available from: <www.microfinanceindia.org/download_reports/state_of_the_sector_report_2010.pdf>

About the authors

Jeffrey Ashe is the director of community finance at Oxfam America. He designed and leads the organization's Saving for Change (SfC) programme, which has grown to 600,000 savings group members in Mali, Senegal, Cambodia, El Salvador, and Guatemala. SfC's design is based on research Jeff carried out in Nepal, India, and Zimbabwe. He previously founded and led Working Capital, which was for a time the largest microfinance institution in the US, and has been a consultant in microfinance projects in more than 30 countries. While at ACCION International he directed the PISCES studies, the first worldwide studies of microfinance. The PISCES studies introduced group lending to ACCION in 1981, marking the ramp-up of ACCION's work in this field. As a Peace Corps Volunteer in the 1960s, Jeff developed the Campesino Leadership Training programme, through which Peace Corps Volunteers and liberation theology priests and nuns helped ensure that those who tilled the land received their just share. He also teaches microfinance at Columbia and Brandeis Universities.

Candace Nelson is an independent writer, trainer, curriculum designer, researcher, and grants manager. At SEEP, Candace co-coordinates the Savings-Led Financial Services Working Group, an inclusive platform for sharing savings group experiences. In 2011, she led the design team for the Arusha Savings Group Summit, the first global meeting of savings group practitioners. From 2009 to 2010, she was a member of an Aga Khan Foundation research team that produced case studies on the integration of savings groups with other development services. As senior technical advisor to Microfinance Opportunities since 2004, she has written financial education curriculum modules, trained trainers in French and Spanish, and designed financial education curricula for a savings group programme with adolescent girls. From 1999 to 2006, she developed and managed a grant programme supporting economic empowerment for women in east Africa on behalf of the McKnight Foundation.

CHAPTER 1
Savings groups and financial inclusion

Joanna Ledgerwood and Alyssa Jethani

This chapter highlights how informal savings groups are an appropriate tool for financial inclusion of poor people, particularly in rural and remote areas. Countering claims that inclusion is defined by participation in the formal financial sector only, savings groups are presented as being at the core of the financial market system.

Financial inclusion has attained a dominant position on the development agenda of policymakers, regulators, multilateral organizations, and development organizations worldwide. Forums such as the Alliance for Financial Inclusion (AFI) and the G-20's Global Partnership for Financial Inclusion, as well as various industry associations and advocacy initiatives, are all discussing how to build more financially inclusive economic systems. With just over half of the world's population still 'unbanked' (Chaia et al., 2009), it is becoming evident that neither the early focus on *microcredit* nor subsequent investments in the broader *microfinance* field have fully met the challenge of financial inclusion. Embracing this goal has led many stakeholders to focus on *financial market systems* and how to make them work better for the poor. With an increased understanding of the financial market system and, more importantly, an acknowledgement of the diverse needs of consumers, the microfinance industry is reexamining its role in contributing to inclusive finance. 'Looking for major impact from a single product or institution type risks overlooking the inherent complexity of livelihoods and financial service needs' (Ledgerwood and Gibson, forthcoming).

Microfinance has historically focused on microfinance institutions (MFIs) reaching scale and sustainability with, predominantly, one product from one type of institution. The market systems approach, on the other hand, acknowledges that there are a diverse range of actors – some providing services directly to consumers, others providing support services to financial service providers themselves, and still others contributing to ensuring an enabling environment – all of whom, together, create the market system. Increasing access to financial services starts with recognizing that the financial market system is complex, and requires greater understanding of how the poor currently use financial tools, how better tools might benefit them, and their barriers to access and usage.

There is now broad consensus that a range of services is needed to meet the many and varied financial service needs of the poor. Stakeholders are also beginning to acknowledge that many of these needs are met by a spectrum of providers, from informal moneylenders and deposit collectors, to development-led initiatives such as savings groups (SGs) and self-help groups (SHGs), to local Savings and Credit Cooperative Societies (SACCOs) and MFIs, to, in some cases, regulated banks. Financial sector surveys such as FinScope, the Global Findex Database, financial diary studies, and others, are showing the significant role that informal and community-based providers play in the financial lives of the poor. Nevertheless, many stakeholders contend that expanding financial inclusion requires bringing the poor into the formal financial system. This raises the question of the role of savings groups in contributing to increased financial inclusion. SGs are one among many options to increase access to financial services (savings, credit, payments, and insurance), meeting an important need not yet filled by the formal sector. But are SG members financially included? We believe that facilitated community-based groups such as SGs are indeed legitimate providers of financial services, and that they contribute to financial inclusion. Furthermore, we contend they play a significant role in developing the financial capabilities of consumers – one of the most important challenges that financial inclusion strategies aim to address. Thus, SGs contribute to financial inclusion by both providing financial services and developing financially capable consumers.

Moreover, SGs can serve as a delivery channel for (or stepping stone toward) more formal services, particularly as technology continues to support broader outreach. SG members can also be linked to formal financial service providers as a means to further expand access and financial inclusion.

This chapter highlights how SGs can contribute to improved financial inclusion through discussion of: 1) financial inclusion and the financial market system; 2) the role of SGs as financial service providers in the market system; 3) the role of facilitating agencies with SGs; 4) the role of SGs in creating financially capable consumers; and 5) linkages of SG members to formal financial services.

Financial inclusion and the financial market system

Full financial inclusion is a state in which all people who can use them have access to a full suite of quality financial services, provided at affordable prices in a convenient manner, and with dignity for the clients. Financial services are delivered by a range of providers, most of them private, and reach everyone who can use them, including disabled, poor and rural populations. (Center for Financial Inclusion at ACCION International, 2010)

Financial inclusion is a multi-dimensional, pro-client concept that encompasses increased access, better products and services, and effective usage. Realizing this concept requires more than institutional expansion and portfolio growth, two goals that drove early development of the microfinance industry (Cohen and Nelson, 2011). It requires a much more nuanced understanding of how the poor manage their financial lives, and what types of providers and services best meet their needs. To make the financial market system work better for the poor, constraints and opportunities to improving financial inclusion, as well the relative benefits and uses of the informal and formal sectors, all need to be understood more fully.

While many MFIs have commercialized, and banks are beginning to serve lower-income women and men, significant market constraints still hamper access to financial services. The microfinance industry's overall outreach remains low; only a small percentage of the population in most countries can access *formal* financial services, while well over 50 per cent of populations remain completely excluded from all financial services. A Financial Access Initiative Framing Note, 'Half the World is Unbanked', states that 2.5 billion adults – just over half of the world's adult population – do not use formal financial services to save or borrow, and that 62 per cent of adults (nearly 2.2 billion) living in Asia, Africa, Latin America, and the Middle East are unserved (Chaia et al., 2009). Furthermore, low rates of loan utilization and dormant deposit accounts among those who have accessed services raise questions about how valuable the poor find microfinance products. In the Global Findex Database, a study conducted by the World Bank in 148 economies, 41 per cent of adults above age 15 in developing economies reported having a formal account compared to 89 per cent of adults in high-income economies – thus highlighting low access to the formal financial sector in lower- and middle-income economies. Of those in developing countries with a formal account, 10 per cent made no deposits or withdrawals from the account in a typical month, illustrating low usage despite access. Nevertheless, there are opportunities to leverage technological advances in mobile services to foster flexibility and convenience for SG members, as well

---

Box 1.1 Financial access trends in Kenya

FinAccess studies in Kenya in 2006 and 2009 show that the number of formally included people (defined as those using a bank, Postbank, or insurance product) went up from 18.9 per cent in 2006 to 22.6 per cent in 2009. Surprisingly, despite the growth in formal inclusion, the number of people also using informal services (especially Rotating Savings and Credit Associations, or ROSCAs, and other community-based groups) increased from 37.5 per cent in 2006 to 38.7 per cent in 2009. Meanwhile, the proportion of financially excluded people has decreased from 38.4 to 32.7 per cent, a decline especially apparent in urban areas, where financial exclusion was halved in three years (42.9 per cent in 2006 to 20.9 per cent in 2009). Savings usage increased in all but the top wealth quintile between 2006 and 2009. Most importantly, savings rates increased in the lowest wealth quintile, from 23 per cent in 2006 to 29 per cent in 2009. While MFIs are still small actors in the Kenyan financial sector, they have doubled their outreach from 1.7 per cent in 2006 to 3.4 per cent in 2009. Accumulating Savings and Credit Associations (ASCAs) are being used more frequently across all income groups; overall membership increased from just under a million people in 2006 to 1.5 million in 2009. These numbers give hope for continued progress, yet remain daunting in their indication of the task that still lies ahead.

Source: Financial Sector Deepening Kenya, 2009

as to increase awareness of other opportunities in the informal sector where the majority of the population transacts. For example, 16 per cent of adults in Sub-Saharan Africa report having used a mobile phone to transact over the past 12 months (Demirguc-Kunt and Klapper, 2012). Progress is possible, though this figure reflects that much more work is necessary in order to increase access to financial services that meet client needs in a meaningful way.

Recent studies compiled in *Portfolios of the Poor* (Collins et al., 2009) highlight how low-income families use a variety of providers and products, both formal and informal, to manage their daily finances. This broader view of financial service use is a first step toward understanding financial markets, and recognizing the legitimate roles and contributions of diverse providers, including savings groups. Though relatively informal, SGs play an active role in the financial market and thus, we argue, those who use them are financially included.

The financial market system[1]

The market systems approach provides a practical means to identify constraints and opportunities to linking the poor with appropriate financial services and delivery channels. The two main sets of functions in market systems include:

- Core: transactions between **providers** and **clients**
- Supporting functions: the collection of functions which provide both the **rules** that shape behaviour and the **information** and **services** that support the development and expansion of the core.

The core of market systems are the transactions between the provider and client – the central function of markets. However, the nature and efficiency of transactions are shaped by a range of other *supporting functions* which provide information, rules, knowledge, and incentives that both determine behaviour and practices, and shape relationships (see Figure 1.1).

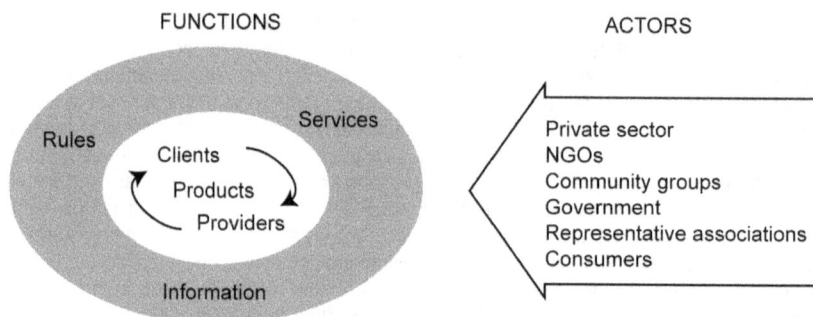

Figure 1.1 Financial market systems framework
Source: Joakim Vincze, adapted from M4P Hub, 2008

Considering the market as a system extends its purview beyond clients (demand) and providers (supply) to other actors who influence transactions, such as government, private sector service providers, associations, and communities. This multi-function, multiple-player arrangement is a 'market system' (M4P Hub, 2008). 'When the combination of functions and players that constitute financial market systems works well, benefits follow; when they do not, benefits for consumers, especially the poor, are likely to be limited and/or transient' (Ledgerwood and Gibson, forthcoming).

Why discuss the financial market system in a book that focuses on savings groups? Because SGs have a place within the system as legitimate providers in the core, alongside MFIs, banks, SACCOs, and others. SGs (the provider) offer their members (clients) savings, credit, and insurance (the products) in small, manageable amounts convenient for poor women and men (see Table 1.1).

Table 1.1 Where savings groups fit in the financial market system

Financial market system – the core		
Providers	Clients	Products
Savings groups	Group members	Savings Loans Insurance

Highlighting how SGs fit within the system and how they fill gaps with services that others have not been able to provide should encourage investments in their facilitation and growth. Furthermore, understanding how other functions, rules, and norms support and motivate poor women and men to utilize community-based services, including SGs, can lead to better-working financial markets.

Donors committed to improving access to financial services benefit from examining the market system, and identifying where they can invest to most effectively realize their objectives. Achieving a fully-inclusive financial system requires an approach that recognizes the different financial service needs among various lower-income segments, as well as the diversity of barriers to access. If we can better understand the constraints to accessing financial services, we may also be better able to identify opportunities to improve access to and usage of these services.

The core – demand and supply

A traditional view of the financial market has the core of the system populated by MFIs, banks, SACCOs, and other more formalized providers. However, an expanded view includes all financial services providers – formal and informal. Full financial inclusion recognizes the breadth of providers and works along the full continuum of market actors to improve access and outreach to the poor (see Figure 1.2).

Community-based   **Institutional**

← —— →

Individuals	Community-based groups	Registered institutions	Regulated institutions
Moneylenders	*Indigenous*: ROSCAs[1], ASCAs[2]	Cooperatives/SACCOs[4]	Deposit-taking MFIs
Deposit collectors	Burial societies / stretcher clubs	NGO MFIs / mutual insurers	Banks
Pawnbrokers	*Facilitated*: self-help groups	Money transfer companies	Credit unions
Traders	Savings groups	Mobile network operators	NBFIs[5]
Shop owners	Financial service associations	Suppliers/wholesalers	Commercial insurers
Friends/family	CVECAs[3]	Post offices	

Note: Banks include state, rural, and savings banks as well as commercial microfinance banks
1 Rotating Savings and Credit Associations
2 Accumulating Savings and Credit Associations
3 *Caisses Villageoises D'épargne et de Crédit Autogérées* (self-reliant village savings and credit banks)
4 Savings and Credit Cooperatives
5 Non-Bank Financial Institutions

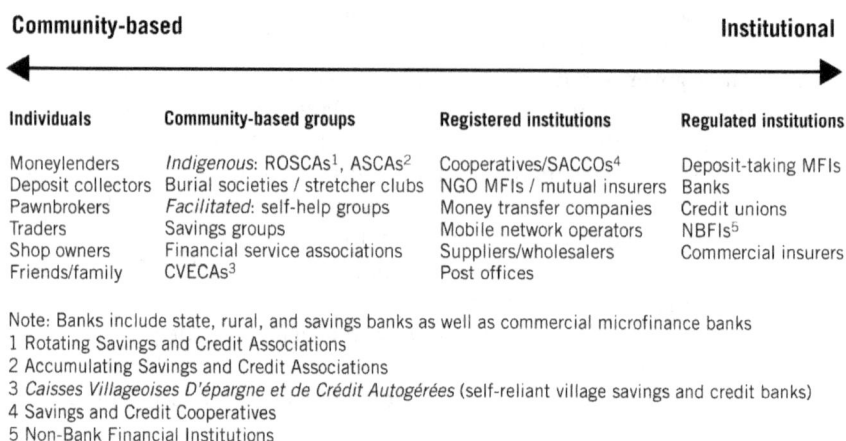

Figure 1.2 Spectrum of financial service providers

By examining the core, stakeholders interested in expanding financial inclusion acknowledge the varied providers and services, and how they each meet different target markets and needs. Savings groups fill the gap between registered, semi-formal institutions such as NGO MFIs and SACCOs, and informal moneylenders, friends, and family who offer financial services. SGs offer an effective means to meet the financial needs of those too poor or in locations too remote to access services from banks or MFIs. In many rural, remote areas, SGs are the only means members have to safely save and conveniently borrow. In addition, the groups provide *flexibility*, with members setting the rules, meeting times, interest rates, and so on; *proximity*, in terms of where the group meets; *reliability*, as the group determines the quality of services; and finally *convenience* – all important needs the microfinance industry is now recognizing.[2] Ideally, as more providers become competitive in rural, remote markets and as financial literacy increases, the poor will have more options of places to save. In the meantime, SGs fill a large gap. While many savers in the developing world blend formal and informal methods, an even larger share uses only community savings clubs. 'In Sub-Saharan Africa 34 per cent of savers report having saved using a community savings club (and not a formal financial institution) in the past 12 months' (Demirguc-Kunt and Klapper, 2012).

SGs also address weaknesses in the informal sector. Unlike ROSCAs, they allow for flexible savings amounts and easy access to loans. While informal burial societies enable members to save for a specific risk, SGs do not dictate what an individual must save for, nor for what she can borrow. The annual distribution of funds allows for greater transparency and trust in the system, in contrast to the more traditional Accumulating Savings and Credit Associations (ASCAs). The easy recordkeeping systems enable group members to each know how much money the group has, while group bylaws reinforce transparency and trust. Transparent elections and rotation of leaders reduce power dynamics in the groups, mitigating the risk of elite capture. Additionally, the social fund introduces the concept of insurance and paying a premium for a service in case of, for example, a health emergency.

While the advantages of SGs may draw members away from other providers, typically moneylenders or MFIs, their limitations can provoke movement in the other direction. Although the small loan sizes are what members often find so useful, they may be too small for someone wanting to make a more substantial productive investment. Furthermore, because group members are often involved in the same economic activities and have children attending the same schools, there can be high demand for loans at the same time (to pay school fees for example) which the SG many not be able to satisfy, thus limiting its effectiveness. Finally, as a commitment savings mechanism, SGs instill the discipline to save, but limit access to accumulated funds during the cycle. Lack of access can be a constraint when either disaster or opportunity knocks at the door.

SGs meet many needs for financial services, but certainly not all of them. As part of the *core*, SGs do not operate in isolation; rather, they are often one of many instruments members use to meet their needs. A member may also participate in a ROSCA for a specific purpose (e.g. to save for iron roofing sheets or a solar lamp) while simultaneously participating in an SG. Members can also become clients of MFIs, where available, to take advantage of different and sometimes complementary services. SG members have used their group savings to qualify for an MFI loan; others 'graduate' to bigger loans from more formal providers; and still others remain active in both. 'Many people use both formal and community-based savings methods, especially in the developing world. In Sub-Saharan Africa 5 per cent of adults (and 14 per cent of savers) report having saved using both formal and community-based methods in the past year. Globally, slightly less than half of all adults who report having saved in the past 12 months using an informal savings club or person outside the family, also report having saved using a formal financial institution' (Demirguc-Kunt and Klapper, 2012).

Supporting functions

Surrounding the core are supporting functions including rules and norms, information, and services that guide the behaviour of consumers and providers. Three key supporting functions for SGs are: the provision of information; access to other service providers including, for example, mobile banking through agent networks; and informal and formal rules.

Access to financial services by poor women and men is affected by a lack of information. In part, usage of formal sector services is hampered by asymmetries of information and power between financial institutions and poor consumers, an imbalance which grows as inexperienced customers choose among increasingly sophisticated products. Negative outcomes can result, due to either institutional abuses or ill-informed client decisions (Cohen and Nelson, 2011). Savings groups address this information imbalance by operating transparently and developing the financial capability of their members through experience, and, in some cases, financial education (discussed later).

Other services such as mobile banking can be harnessed to strengthen SGs. Rapidly growing access to mobile phones, even in remote areas, provides an opportunity for members to contribute savings or make loan payments when they cannot attend a meeting. Where mobile networks are available, groups are beginning to explore the opportunities for safeguarding excess funds by storing them on a mobile phone. Individual members are doing the same. For example, if a member cannot attend the group meeting, she can send her savings contribution (share purchases) or make a loan payment via mobile money, whereby a mobile phone and/or agent is used to transfer funds to and from the savings group.

Both formal and informal rules can affect the functioning of SGs. SG members are particularly affected by informal rules including gender, age, and even caste dynamics. While cultural norms often work to exclude the poor

---

Box 1.2 In Tanzania, CARE and Vodacom help savings groups use M-Pesa

CARE partnered with Vodacom in late 2010 to introduce group-based M-Pesa accounts on a pilot basis to VSLAs in three northern districts. As of December 2010, CARE and Vodacom Tanzania have trained 39 VSLAs on the use of M-Pesa as a stand-alone 'savings' product, and by April 2011, all had opened group M-Pesa accounts. One new M-Pesa agent was also created at the urging of the pilot VSLAs. Groups can verify the balance in their accounts during meetings, ensuring transparency of funds. In addition, some VSLAs are using their M-Pesa accounts to save for the bulk purchase of agricultural inputs.

As of April 2011, there had been 72 deposit transactions of a total value of US$8,388, and 49 withdrawal transactions totalling $4,852. The average balance on M-Pesa accounts is $126.90. Since the partnership launched, many more groups outside the three targeted districts have approached Vodacom and opened VSLA group accounts with M-Pesa, without having received any training or sensitization from CARE on the M-Pesa product.

Several challenges were encountered during the initial implementation, however, and understanding these challenges will help other money wallet providers understand how to interact with groups and individuals in remote locations. Lessons include:

- Education on the product, including its costs and opportunities, requires an upfront investment as well as time. However, once group members know how the system works and what its benefits are, word of mouth spreads and the next round of users requires less training.
- The availability and placement of M-Pesa agents is crucial to reach vast numbers of people. VSLA members can help identify new agents in their local community.
- The availability of cash holdings in small bills is key in rural areas, where the number of transactions may be high, but transaction amounts are small.

Source: Invested Development, 2012; Hendricks and Chidiac, 2011

or otherwise disadvantaged from accessing formal providers, as autonomous, community-based institutions, SGs work within cultural norms as inclusively as possible. In many areas, women-only SGs help to reduce negative effects of gender dynamics. Some groups work to reduce caste barriers or age-specific issues that discriminate against the young and old alike. SGs attempt to prevent elite capture through transparent operations and fair election processes. Group members develop discipline (e.g. regular meeting attendance, timely arrival, weekly share purchases) and follow the group rules, giving them experience with the advantages and disadvantages of the rules and norms required to engage with financial service providers. The SG constitution and bylaws provide enforcement muscle (albeit informal) to reduce asymmetries of information. The participatory process of developing rules with regards to interest rates, lending ratios, social fund contributions, fines, and fees, encourages equal and transparent access to information.

Savings groups are clearly not the only solution leading to increased financial inclusion – and indeed, no single type of financial institution can be. But if and when members' financial service and/or investment needs grow beyond their SGs' capacity, MFIs gain clients who are well-versed in the principles of saving and prudential management of household finances. The coexistence of multiple financial service providers in the system, formal and informal, contributes to a more inclusive market.

Where do facilitating agencies fit in a market systems framework?

Facilitating agencies (FAs) play a unique role in improving the market system to work better for the poor. Working outside the system itself, facilitators are not permanent market players and by definition must develop a vision of how the system will work once they leave. In the case of SGs, facilitating agencies work primarily to expand the core of the market system, where SGs are positioned (see Figure 1.3).

In the world of savings groups, facilitating agencies are the external entities, typically international or local NGOs, that introduce and catalyze a process of group formation and operation that often becomes self-replicating. Facilitating agencies mobilize, train, and support savings groups, usually through their first cycle of saving and lending, culminating in share-out. As promoters of SGs, the role of facilitating agencies is to increase financial inclusion by expanding the core – that is, by developing more SGs.

Facilitating agencies serve as temporary training agencies (and in most cases, replicators). They do not seek to provide financial services directly themselves; rather, their primary goal is to facilitate the establishment of sustainable financial service providers (SGs) that meet the needs of poor consumers. Facilitation of SGs is a good example of a development initiative that sustainably improves the financial market system. The role of facilitating agencies working with SGs is to train groups to manage their own transactions independently. Facilitators must have an exit strategy and

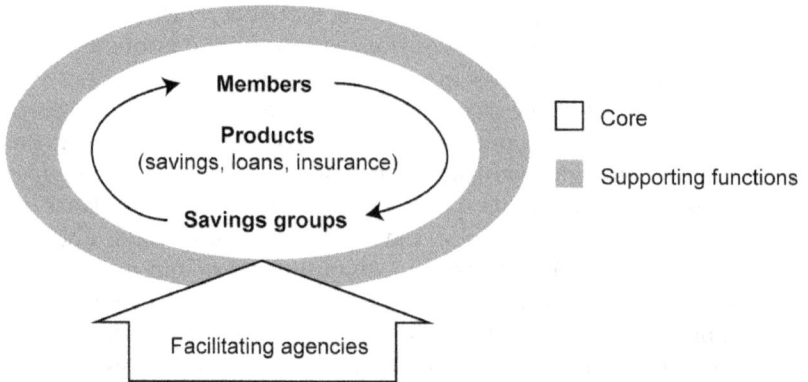

Figure 1.3 Facilitating agencies of savings groups
Source: Joakim Vincze, adapted from M4P Hub, 2008

clearly think through how the system can and should function without their presence. One of the key tenets of the market systems approach is sustainability – not just sustainability of the groups themselves, but sustainability of ongoing access to savings groups and their continued expansion without facilitating agencies.

FAs provide the link to public and private donors whose support for SGs makes an important contribution to financial inclusion. Similar to subsidies that are provided to start MFIs and develop their capacity, donor funds subsidize the formation of SGs. Once established, like many MFIs, SGs operate independently. The key to justifying this up-front investment is reasonable cost at the outset, and reasonable expectations for SGs to remain in the market as providers once facilitating agencies leave.

As discussed in Chapter 3, fee-for-service training is emerging as the future of the movement. Some facilitating agencies focus on developing a cadre of trusted, trained local agents who interact regularly with groups, providing support, linkages, and even extra trainings either voluntarily or for a fee. Other facilitating agencies are learning from experiences such as the SHG movement in India, which has achieved significant scale with the help of partnerships and aligned incentives with the private sector. FAs continue to research and experiment to achieve scale and sustainability at the lowest cost possible – and with an exit strategy in mind.

As is evidenced by the experience of CARE and CRS, facilitating agencies have a significant role to play in determining how to best ensure ongoing access to savings groups at scale (see Box 1.3 and Chapter 3).

Box 1.3 Establishing sustainable service delivery

Experience in East Africa is pointing toward the spread of a fee-for-service model in which new groups pay trainers to help them learn how to form and operate a savings group. In Kenya, the Financial Sector Deepening project (FSDK), seeking to reach at least two million Kenyans with savings groups over the next ten years, partnered with CARE to pilot a novel approach: the use of franchisees who would contract their own community-based trainers (CBTs) to mobilize and train SGs in return for a fee per successful group trained. The pilot reached well over double the target (more than 100,000 people) while dramatically reducing the cost per member trained. Communities not reached during the project are now slowly agreeing to pay the trainers to help them get their own SGs up and running. Initially people have resisted paying for a service that was provided for free to their neighbours; thus, demand and income have been much lower than expected. However, those involved predict that business will pick up because savings groups are now well-known and in demand. New entrants want help forming SGs, and old groups often seek intermittent assistance even after graduation.

In East Africa, Catholic Relief Services is piloting a model to develop a private commercial system for training and supporting SGs. Hired field agents spend one year on salary learning how to perform their duties. After a rigorous certification process, these agents become Private Service Providers (PSPs). The communities they work in are prepared from the beginning for the eventuality that they will assume the responsibility to pay the PSP. CRS has established a network of trainers to provide peer-maintained quality assurance.

While fee-for-service seems like the logical next step from a market development perspective, several questions arise:

1. If groups self-replicate, will there be a sufficient market for training services in the longer term? Will they need more than modest inputs from external support providers over time?
2. If SG replication proves robust, will it be cheaper to simply invest in building a critical mass of SGs, and rely on a combination of spontaneous fee-for-service and voluntary replication?

Source: Ferrand, 2011

How do savings groups contribute to creating financially capable consumers?

So far, we have argued that financial inclusion requires accessible and appropriate products from diverse providers. We have also argued for the acknowledgement of the various functions and actors of the financial market system, and the role of SGs within that system. As part of this system, financial inclusion also requires *financially capable* consumers who not only understand basic information about financial products and services, but can apply that knowledge to make informed decisions and take effective actions regarding the management of their money (Staschen and Nelson, forthcoming). Savings groups provide an optimal opportunity for members to learn how to manage savings and loans (and in some cases, insurance) in a relatively safe and reliable environment. Group members learn by doing.[3] They keep records of their individual transactions; at annual share-out they see how much their money 'grows' (savings plus accumulated interest) by the end of the cycle. They learn how to determine safe amounts to borrow; many group constitutions specify a lending-to-savings ratio (typically 3:1) to reduce over-indebtedness and the risk of default. These SG processes are designed to be simple, clear to all, and transparent – qualities that may not always exist with products offered by institutional providers.

Box 1.4 Savings groups and financial capability

From observations of CRS savings groups in Central America and Kenya, Suzanne Andrews writes that she is confident participation in savings groups promotes financial capability, the practical objective of any financial literacy programme. Regular meetings keep financial management at the front of members' minds, leading them to think critically about their fiscal behaviour. Members support one another to save more and to access loans when there is an investment opportunity or need, and to share financial advice. The groups organically create a de facto tailored financial education programme.

Improving daily financial management. First the obvious: savings groups keep members focused on opportunities to save. Members in diverse groups and settings from Guatemala to Kenya are quick to list the small sacrifices they have made to increase their savings: walking to save bus fare, bringing snacks from home, buying in bulk, and reducing unnecessary purchases. And members across the globe list similar benefits from accessing loans and their accumulated savings at share-out, using the funds to grow their businesses, pay school fees, improve their homes, and cover emergency expenses.

Critically analyzing financial tools. Participation in savings groups also helps members to re-evaluate their use of other financial services and products. In one community in Kenya where microcredit penetration is quite high, and many savings group members were formerly in credit groups, members encourage one another to leave MFI credit groups and rely instead on savings group credit, keeping the profits within the community. In some villages, MFI presence has declined dramatically.

Diversifying savings products. While scepticism toward MFI microcredit is pervasive among group members, many have diversified their savings strategy since joining the group by combining group savings with formal bank accounts. In Kenya, one woman opened a youth savings account for her granddaughter following share-out. She explained that while the bank account offers a lower return, it provides a more secure form of insurance in case something happens to her. In one village in Honduras, some members funnelled their accumulated savings into a credit union savings account after share-out. They explained that while they appreciated the regular deposits and access to loans in the savings group, they perceived the credit union as more secure for long-term savings. At the time [Andrews] visited this particular group, the members were planning to open a group account to secure surplus (un-lent) savings in their second year.

Where alternative savings and credit products are available, accessible (with a reasonable fee structure and low minimum deposit), and secure, savvy savings group members will diversify their savings and compare credit terms, abandoning credit schemes that are higher-cost or less convenient. Where they are not, members will frequently look for ways to maximize the financial benefits of the group by increasing their savings, taking loans when necessary, and trading business tips with other members. Thus, over time, group members optimize their financial management in a way that can surely be recognized as increased financial capability.

Source: Andrews, 2011

Managing money is a continually evolving and challenging process, particularly for poor women and men who often have unpredictable or seasonal incomes. Through their participation in SGs, members have an opportunity to save, borrow and spend wisely, generate more stable cash flows, and manage the challenges associated with costly unexpected and expected life cycle events. Facing challenges among group members with similar issues can reinforce social support and safety nets, as well as allow members to learn from each other, further developing their financial capabilities.

Financial capabilities can also contribute to effective consumer protection. Consumer protection requires the engagement of multiple players, one of which is an empowered base of consumers who can participate in their own protection. Financial education can further support this goal, as it enables clients to develop relationships with financial service providers on the basis of knowledge and choice as opposed to fear (Staschen and Nelson, forthcoming). In savings groups, the group itself facilitates such relationships. Social solidarity creates a safe environment for members to develop a relationship with their provider – the group itself – with fewer direct and indirect costs (loss of collateral, embarrassment, etc.), particularly as they learn how the group functions and how to use its different products. Thus, the SG methodology embodies the principles of consumer protection now widely advocated across the microfinance industry: transparency, fair treatment, self-regulation, and voluntary codes of conduct and principles.[4] These principles encourage more financially inclusive, sustainable markets. In an environment of increasingly complex financial products and services, effective consumer protection and financially capable consumers are important for the overall sustainability of the financial market system (Staschen and Nelson, forthcoming).

Financial education

The Center for Financial Inclusion publication 'Opportunities and Obstacles to Financial Inclusion' (Gardeva and Rhyne, 2011) highlights a number of strategies to expand inclusion, such as savings groups and self-help groups. One of the most significant findings from the survey relates to financial literacy, identified as the number-one constraint to financial inclusion; financial education was identified as the number one-opportunity (Gardeva and Rhyne, 2011).

Although SG membership in and of itself can improve financial capability, some FAs believe they can (and should) do more to improve financial capabilities, and therefore financial inclusion. Financial education is one strategy they are exploring.[5] While still in their early days, training modules on financial education are proving to be very beneficial. The Aga Khan Foundation's Community-based Savings Group programme in Bihar, India, provides financial education to all group members; the programme, which uses storytelling, is designed specifically for non-literate populations. While the impact of the training is currently being assessed, early indications (high demand for the trainings, from non-members as well) suggest that the training is useful to the community. Initial observations indicate that members' savings and loan behaviour are improving; saving amounts have increased, and loans are being effectively utilized.

Financial education is a tool to build financial capability. 'It introduces people to good money management practices with respect to earning, spending, saving, borrowing, and investing' beyond what consumers are learning as they participate in SGs, and 'enables people to shift from reactive to proactive decision-making' (Staschen and Nelson, forthcoming). There is a natural fit, therefore, between financial education and SGs. In the context of savings groups, financial education can:

- increase members' knowledge of how to manage money by giving them access to small loans and lump sums that were not available to them prior to joining an SG;
- enable SG members to plan for future expenses and the use of money received during the share-out;
- allow members to better compare products – a critical skill for all, but especially for those members who gain access to formal MFIs and banks – and to improve their ability to utilize financial services to help achieve their goals; and
- help members to fully understand the costs and benefits of the various forms of mobile money and electronic wallets to which they will increasingly have access.

SGs are a unique platform for financial education training because members can put what they learn into practice right away. Experience is the key to fully understanding how to use and benefit from financial services.

Numerous channels for delivering financial education – including face-to-face training during the SG meeting, traditional stories told with a financial education twist, print and mass media, and established community education programmes – all offer FAs options for tailoring the curriculum to the context and target market, and for crafting the best-quality education tools at the lowest cost.

Linkage to formal financial service providers

As discussed, savings groups do not meet all the financial service needs of their members, nor are they designed to. Some of the limitations of SGs can be addressed by formal financial service providers. This is where understanding the financial market system, including consumer needs, is useful. For example, second- or third-cycle groups that have accumulated large sums of money may choose to deposit excess funds into a bank or other regulated provider. Some group members may want larger loans or want loans for longer terms than the group is able to provide, while other members may want longer- or shorter-term savings products, or specialized insurance products. As a result of

---

Box 1.5 Girls embrace savings groups in Burundi

In a small village in central Burundi, 25 teenage girls stand in a single-file line, eagerly awaiting their training agent's next word. 'Water!' she says. Most of the girls in line quickly step to their left; one steps to her right. To this girl, the training agent asks, 'Did you understand the word? I said "water"! If you think that it is a need, step to your left. If you think it is a want, step to your right!'

'I understood you!' the lone rebel replies, smiling broadly. 'And for me, water is a want. I don't need it to live. I could drink beer every day and never have water again!' The girls erupt into laughter and quickly challenge her answer.

The scene is a financial education learning session on 'distinguishing between wants and needs;' the girls are members of a savings group in Burundi, part of CARE's first attempt to introduce the SG model to teenage girls. As of May 2011, Burundi has over 600 savings groups with a collective 12,500 members, all girls aged 14–22. These groups provide girls with financial education in addition to a place to save and lend. Though often filled with laughter and entertaining moments, training sessions provide girls a chance to discuss basic but critical financial decisions for which they have never received any guidance.

Tasked with developing the financial education curriculum for these groups, Microfinance Opportunities (MFO) drafted modules on four distinct themes: saving, debt management, earning money, and talking about money. From these themes, CARE chose to focus on savings. Why savings, one might ask, when the girls are learning how to save in the context of their savings groups? Through the curriculum the girls learn strategies to save, maximizing their participation in the groups and giving their savings activities a clear purpose. The girls learned the 'Seven Strategies of Saving', around which they created chants and songs that have helped both to make the strategies integral to the group culture, and to advertise them more broadly. Other CARE staff, including drivers and security guards, ask to learn about the seven strategies of saving.

Group members elected by their peers are trained to lead the learning sessions with their respective groups. This peer training model was chosen for its low cost and long-term sustainability.

Although the *Ishaka* girls also received training on sexuality and human rights, they accord priority to financial education. As they explained, knowing how to protect themselves against pregnancy and HIV/AIDs is not enough. Having the financial means enables the girls to say 'no' and that is what has truly made a difference in their ability to be proactive about their health.

Observing these meetings, it is clear that the savings aspect draws these girls in and holds them together, but the financial education component of the programme is getting them talking about their hopes, their dreams, and their financial futures.

Source: Nelson and Butzberger, 2011

---

this emerging demand, facilitating agencies are debating the merits of linking SGs to formal financial service providers. Advocates suggest SGs are one step on the ladder to formal financial inclusion, while others are concerned about elite capture and the sustainability of linked groups. These debates centre on the following questions:

- Should linkages be created for the purposes of savings, credit, or both?
- Should FAs focus on linking individual members only, or should they pursue strategies that link the whole group to formal financial institutions?

- Should FAs 'graduate' SGs to the formal sector? Or is there a way to preserve the original group and its characteristics while simultaneously fostering new relationships with other providers?
- What is the role and responsibility of the FA in financial literacy and consumer protection as it fosters such linkages?

SGs have been linked to other financial service providers for savings, credit, and in some cases, insurance products. With savings, the main purpose is to safeguard excess liquidity. For loan capital and insurance, SGs can serve as the delivery channel for external providers such as MFIs, banks, or insurance providers. In these instances, the transaction can take place either directly at a branch or through a field officer, or indirectly through an ATM, over a mobile phone, or through an agent with a card and point-of-sale device.

Linkages for excess liquidity

Leading innovation in financial linkages, CARE strongly believes that any financial inclusion strategy for savings groups cannot ignore the formal financial sector: 'CARE's strategy for financial inclusion is to look at [savings groups] as the foundation and a basic and often necessary first step to move the excluded into the financial system. In CARE's savings-led approach, linkage to formal financial institutions is also savings-led and the continued importance of savings is emphasized throughout the linkage process' (Hendricks and Chidiac, 2011).

As group savings balances increase, some SGs and facilitating agencies have become concerned about the safety of funds and look to formal financial service providers to deposit excess liquidity when such a facility, either a bank branch or an agent with a mobile phone, is available at a reasonable distance.

One of the current challenges groups face when making deposits in an external institution is the lack of ownership over the money to be deposited. Regulated institutions do not always have the capacity to offer group accounts for informal, non-registered groups; therefore, members are often forced to rely on one or two individuals in the group to open the account, with the resulting risk of elite capture and reduced transparency. However, some groups have found innovative ways to address these issues (see boxes 1.6–1.8).

Box 1.6 Spontaneous bank linkages with savings groups promoted by Peace Corps in Ecuador

The Peace Corps recommends that members keep their savings in a cashbox with three locks and three keys. It does not provide guidance on how to open a group savings account at a financial institution. Eleven years into the programme, groups had, of their own accord, opened individual or group savings accounts with local, formal financial institutions. Half of the SGs (called community banks) keep their money in a locked box, while the other half keep their money in a financial institution.

Source: Fleischer Proaño et al., 2010

Box 1.7 MSDSP Tajikistan pilots a creative way to keep savings safe

To address security concerns of SGs in their second or third cycle, or near the end of a cycle when group funds often reach a considerable sum, the Mountain Societies Development Support Programme (MSDSP) piloted linkages of SGs to Ahmonatbank, a savings bank in Tajikistan.

An officer from Ahmonatbank's district office visits each linked SG to observe its meetings. Upon completion of the SG meeting, the officer explains how the group could save in the bank, what fees are required to withdraw money, and what penalties will be assigned if money is withdrawn before three months. If interested, the group nominates one individual under which the bank account can be registered. Only one member can deposit and withdraw money on the group's behalf, because unregistered groups (such as SGs) cannot open a group bank account. MSDSP is working to mitigate this potential risk to the group. The bank representative facilitates an informal agreement between the group and the individual to ensure safety of the funds. When deposits are made, a receipt is issued and entered in the savings book. The receipt and the savings book are then locked in the group cash box. At the end of each meeting, the group recounts the amount in the bank in addition to the standard sums. In addition, two members are required to withdraw funds.

Source: Jethani, 2011

To date, a relatively small number of savings groups have used accounts for excess liquidity. However, as facilitating agencies and the SGs they support continue to experiment, innovate, and learn in this area, good practice guidelines are beginning to emerge.

Box 1.8 CARE, Equity Bank, and Orange use mobile phones to connect savings groups to banks

A recent partnership among CARE, Equity Bank, and Orange allows CARE Village Savings and Loans Associations (VSLAs) to open an Equity Bank account and deposit cash into interest-bearing group savings accounts without visiting a physical branch. This is made possible by the extensive network of Equity Bank/Orange agents throughout Kenya.

To ensure account security, CARE, Orange, and Equity Bank developed a first-of-its-kind security verification system that requires three VSLA members to provide PINs for every transaction – the electronic equivalent of the three-padlock VSLA metal lockbox that prevents any one person from accessing the group's cash. Although individuals have accessed bank accounts with mobile phones before, this is the first system that allows groups the same type of secure mobile access.

All group members can register their mobile phones, enabling them to receive an SMS announcing any transaction made to the group account. This system ensures that no one can tamper with the group's resources between meetings.

Equity Bank's Pamoja savings account offers a safe place to save, a 2.5 per cent annual interest rate, no account maintenance or deposit fees, and minimal withdrawal fees. VSLAs will have 24-hour access to their accounts using the Eazzy 24/7 mobile phone platform. Using the same system, Equity will soon offer loans to VSLAs. CARE and its partners have already facilitated the product with 25 interested VSLAs, hoping to scale up to 175 groups in six months. If the initial launch is successful, Equity/Orange mobile bank accounts will be made available to all CARE-affiliated savings groups in Kenya.

Source: CARE, 2012

Linkages for external loan capital

As group members demand capital beyond the capacity of their SGs, facilitating agencies feel a responsibility to facilitate mutually beneficial partnerships, ensuring consumer protection principles along the way. CARE, for example, has spent a significant amount of time working with policy frameworks to smooth the transition for savings groups accessing formal financial services. Regulatory frameworks in many countries, however, make it difficult for banks and SGs to link; some governments require SGs to first register as cooperatives, risking a potential compromise with their autonomy and simplicity. Formalization may also reduce some of the advantages SGs have in transparency, costs, trust, and other aspects. Therefore, CARE advocates for a simple, local registration process that allows the group to maintain its simple structure and governance models (Hendricks and Chidiac, 2011).

Good practice guidelines for linkage to external loan capital

How savings groups should be linked to external, formal financial institutions remains a topic of debate. CARE, a major proponent of linkage, advocates linking the group (rather than individual members) to the bank. It

---

Box 1.9 Wholesale lending to savings groups in Niger

The SG methodology was first put into practice in 1991 in Niger, and evolved under CARE's Mata Masu Dumbara ('Women Moving Forward' in the Hausa language) programme. In 2008, the programme had at least 150,000 members, when a half-dozen financial institutions – both MFIs and credit unions – began lending to the groups (without CARE's knowledge or facilitation). The lenders made loans to the group and used group assets as collateral. Loans were disbursed, usually in the lender's office, to the group president and treasurer, often the same two members who had signed the contract.

After initial success, portfolios declined and defaults increased. CARE commissioned two studies to further investigate the linkage programmes and found an estimated 40 per cent of groups that had received loans were having difficulties repaying them. Furthermore, most of those who agreed to take out a first loan declined to take subsequent ones. The groups that did not take out any loans gained an average of 4.5 members, while the groups that did take out loans lost members. Several factors that explain these findings are listed below:

- Financial institutions were making large loans, leveraging as much as ten times the total savings of the groups.
- Loans required monthly repayments with no flexibility in case the group had difficulties.
- Groups were not well-prepared to understand the implications of taking on external debt.
- The external loan was a parallel financial obligation with no relationship to the existing savings and borrowing activities of the group.
- Groups were receiving multiple loans. In the study sample, groups had an average of four loans from two institutions, often simultaneously.
- Coordination among the lenders was ad hoc and unreliable.
- Loans were being given in a perfunctory fashion with little or no loan analysis.

Source: Rippey, 2011

recommends that financial institutions lend to the group as a whole, arguing that it is more appropriate for the SG to receive a lump sum loan into its fund pool. When external loan funds are co-mingled with the group savings, they can be distributed in the same manner, maintaining group cohesion while enhancing members' financial skills (Hendricks and Chidiac, 2011).

Other facilitating agencies believe that it is unwise to force those who do not want additional loan capital to be jointly liable for those who do. Why put the savings of all group members at risk if one or two default on their loans? Early experiences with bank linkages in Rwanda, Niger, and Malawi demonstrated that this risk was significant (See Box 1.9). SHGs in India have also experienced problems with bank linkages, including elite capture and group collapse as a result of too much capital and decreased incentives to continue saving once external credit was secured. Yet in remote, rural areas, enlisting individual group members as clients is more costly for banks than enlisting a group.

To guide its active pursuit of linkages with formal finance, CARE has developed the following principles (Hendricks and Chidiac, 2011):

Minimum age of groups for linkage is one year – preferably two to three years: Linkage should be a graduation step for qualifying SGs. Most SG members have limited demand for large amounts of credit when they first join. It is only once household finances are stabilized, small-scale income-generating activities have grown a bit, and financial skills have been gained, that groups are ready and able to take on outside debt.

Linkage is not automatic – it must be demand-driven and performance-based: Linkage to an external financial institution must be determined by member demand for additional resources and overall group performance. A group that experiences high default rates or is unable to conduct their share-out without external help is not ready for the added responsibility of external capital. CARE has developed a readiness assessment tool to analyse the groups' ability to take on credit from an external financial institution. Linkages to individual members rather than the group itself must be demand-driven as well. In this case, however, the overall group performance is not as important as the individual's record of savings and loan activity.

Define a maximum debt-to-equity ratio: CARE recommends a maximum debt-to-equity ratio of 3-to-1 for SGs. In the absence of this limit, over-indebtedness has led to default and group dissolution. If individuals are linked for loans, the leverage ratio is determined by the lending institution and is normally based on the individual member's debt capacity and predicted cash flows.

Balloon repayments: CARE recommends that group loans are repaid in one balloon payment, due at the time of the scheduled share-out, because a traditional monthly or biweekly repayment schedule slowly de-capitalizes the group throughout the lending cycle. Interest can be repaid monthly or biweekly.

Limit collateral deposits: Some financial institutions require mandatory savings deposits before loans can be made, both to encourage a savings culture and as collateral for the outstanding loan. However, SGs already have a savings culture and an existing savings pool that acts as collateral for the loan. Forced savings with no or little return can serve as a disincentive to members' future saving or borrowing. The groups' existing financial records of past experience managing their finances should therefore count toward their financial history, and reduce the required compensating balance.

Conclusion and questions for further study

To increase financial inclusion, we need to challenge ourselves to look for models that increase access to appropriate, affordable, and convenient services. These services should provide choice to consumers, allow individuals to manage their cash flows, and help them to plan and invest in a better future. Savings groups meet needs that other providers do not, while at the same time contributing to the development of financially capable consumers. They also operate in the informal sector where the majority of consumers interact. When considering financial inclusion, we need to understand the full market system for financial services and the various functions and actors that play a part in the system – including SGs. We need to continue to examine partnerships and innovations, and better understand the evolving constraints and opportunities in the financial market system. By acknowledging SGs as a legitimate provider, we can justify investments in developing a network of SGs without the ongoing need for facilitating agencies and donor funding. However, some areas require further exploration to fully expand financial inclusion through savings groups:

1. How can we use technology to further meet the needs of SGs and SG members?
2. How do we best encourage consumer protection, particularly among populations with low literacy and financial literacy levels?
3. How do we facilitate increased access to and usage of financial services using SGs and other providers? Innovations through technology or partnerships? Linkages? Financial education?
4. How can we leverage the unique position of SGs to develop more financially capable consumers?

Acknowledgements

The authors are grateful for comments on earlier versions received from Jeffrey Ashe, Candace Nelson, Kim Wilson, Laura Fleischer Proaño, marc bavois, Megan Gash, Katherine Younker, Sybil Chidiac, Noel da'Cruz, Anthony O. Mang'eni, Guy Vanmeenen, Ole Dahl Rasmussen, and Ishmael Kwesi Otchere, and input from Joakim Vincze. Errors of omission or commission remain their own.

Notes

1. The market system approach and its application to financial markets draw directly from the M4P Hub publications. More information is available at: <www.m4phub.org>.
2. For example, *Portfolios of the Poor* identified key principles for developing financial products for the poor, including convenience, flexibility, reliability, and structure (Collins et al., 2009).
3. Some facilitating agencies combine SG facilitation with financial literacy tools and training, further contributing to members' financial capabilities.
4. See GPFI White Paper *Global Standard-Setting Bodies and Financial Inclusion for the Poor*, which states that in low-income jurisdictions, these basic principles (transparent pricing, fair treatment, and effective recourse and dispute resolution) should be prioritized. Retrieved from: <www.cgap.org/sites/default/files/CGAP-White-Paper-Global-Standard-Setting-Bodies-Sep-2011.pdf>
5. Although most of these experiments to date have been with SG programmes for youth, their success has spawned similar results among adult programmes. CARE Burundi is one case in point. FSD Kenya has conducted market research among SGs to determine the broad outlines of a possible financial education curriculum.

References

Andrews, S. (2011) 'Savings groups and financial capability' [blog] <http://savings-revolution.org/blog/2011/11/29/savings-groups-and-financial-capability.html> (posted 29 November).

CARE (2012) 'CARE, Equity Bank and Orange launch partnership to connect community savings groups to banks using mobile phones', March 16, Nairobi. Retrieved from: <www.care.org/newsroom/articles/2012/03/care-mobile-banking-services-kenya-20120316.asp>

Center for Financial Inclusion at ACCION International (2010) 'Financial inclusion: What's the vision?' Center for Financial Inclusion, Washington, D.C. Retrieved from: <www.centerforfinancialinclusion.org/publications-a-resources/browse-publications/216-financial-inclusion-whats-the-vision>

Chaia, A., Dalal, A., Goland, T., Gonzalez, M. J., Morduch, J., and Schiff, R. (2009) 'Half the world is unbanked', Financial Access Initiative Framing Note, New York. Retrieved from: <http://financialaccess.org/sites/default/files/110109%20HalfUnbanked_0.pdf>

Cohen, M. and Nelson, C. (2011) 'Financial literacy: A step for clients towards financial inclusion', commissioned workshop paper presented at the Global Microcredit Summit, Valladolid, Spain, 14–17 November. Retrieved from: <www.globalmicrocreditsummit2011.org/userfiles/file/Workshop%20Papers/M_%20Cohen%20-%20Financial%20Literacy.pdf>

Collins, D., Morduch, J., Rutherford, S. and Ruthven, O. (2009) *Portfolios of the Poor: How the Poor Live on $2 a Day*, Princeton University Press, Princeton, NJ.

Demirguc-Kunt, A. and Klapper, L. (2012) 'Measuring financial inclusion: The Global Findex Database', Policy Research Working Paper Series 6025, The World Bank, Washington, D.C.

Ferrand, D. (2011) 'Keynote paper 1: Strengthening financial service markets', presented at M4P Hub Conference, Brighton, 7–9 November.

Financial Sector Deepening Kenya (2009) 'Financial inclusion in Kenya' [website], <www.fsdkenya.org/finaccess/finaccess.php> [accessed 26 September 2012].

Fleischer Proaño, L., Gash, M., and Kuklewiez, A. (2010). 'Strengths, weaknesses and evolution of the Peace Corps' 11-year old savings group program in Ecuador', Freedom from Hunger Research Report No. 13, FFH, Davis, CA.

Gardeva, A., and Rhyne, E. (2011) 'Opportunities and obstacles to financial inclusion: Survey report'. Retrieved from: <http://centerforfinancialinclusionblog.files.wordpress.com/2011/07/opportunities-and-obstacles-to-financial-inclusion_110708_final.pdf>

Gibson, A. (forthcoming) 'The evolving financial landscape', in J. Ledgerwood (ed.), *The New Microfinance Handbook*, The World Bank, Washington, D.C.

Hendricks, L. and Chidiac, S. (2011) 'Village savings and loans: A pathway to financial inclusion for Africa's poorest households', *Enterprise Development and Microfinance*, 22(2):134–46.

Invested Development (2012) 'Improving informal savings groups with mobile technology', Research Brief, Spring, Invested Development, Nairobi and Boston, MA. Retrieved from: <http://investeddevelopment.com/wp-content/uploads/2012/05/Improving-Informal-Savings-Groups-with-Mobile-Technology.pdf>

Jethani, A. (2011) 'MSDSP Tajikistan pilots a creative way to keep savings safe' [blog] <http://savings-revolution.org/blog/2011/10/27/msdsp-tajikistan-pilots-a-creative-way-to-keep-savings-safe.html> (posted 27 October).

M4P Hub (2008) 'A synthesis for making markets work for the poor (M4P) approach', M4P Hub, Swiss Agency for Development and Cooperation, Bern. Retrieved from: <www.m4phub.org/resource-finder/result.aspx?k=m4p%20synthesis&t=0&c=0&s=0>.

Nelson, C. and Butzberger, B. (2011) 'Savings, financial education, and social support for adolescent girls', Burundi process documentation, CARE Burundi, unpublished.

Rippey, P. (2011) 'Desk review: Three studies and one policy statement concerning wholesale lending to savings groups', AKF Savings Group Learning Initiative, AKF Geneva.

Staschen, N. and Nelson, C. (forthcoming) 'Policy and responsible finance', in J. Ledgerwood (ed.), *The New Microfinance Handbook*, The World Bank, Washington, D.C.

About the authors

Joanna Ledgerwood joined the Aga Khan Foundation in 2007 and leads their Access to Finance activities from the Head Office in Geneva, including overseeing AKF's savings group programmes globally. Before moving to Geneva, Joanna spent six years in Kampala, Uganda, providing support to MFIs seeking to become regulated deposit-taking institutions. She also worked for two years in the Philippines with rural banks, to deepen their outreach to poor men and women. She has written and contributed to numerous papers and books, including *Transforming MFIs* with Victoria White (2006) and the *Microfinance Handbook* (1998), both published by the World Bank. She is writing the *New Microfinance Handbook, A Financial Market System Perspective*, to be published in 2013.

Alyssa Jethani worked as a Program Associate at Aga Khan Foundation's (AKF) headquarters in Geneva, Switzerland, for two years, supporting AKF's access to finance and market development initiatives globally. In particular, she has supported economic livelihoods projects in crafts development and vocational training in Egypt, access to finance assessments in Mozambique, Kyrgyz Republic, and Tajikistan, and a qualitative evaluation of a Savings Group and financial literacy programme in India. Alyssa also worked with AKF's Community-based Savings Group programme, which is currently implemented in seven countries. A graduate of political science and international studies at Yale University, Alyssa is currently completing an MBA at the Yale School of Management, with a focus on private sector development.

CHAPTER 2
Savings group outreach and membership

Susan Johnson and Silvia Storchi

This chapter examines the extent to which savings groups reach remote, poor, and marginalized people, including particular programmes targeted at young people, orphans and vulnerable children, and those living with HIV/AIDS. It covers the issues that arise in replicating the SG model and shows that groups adjust the methodology to suit their needs.

Savings groups are an appropriate tool for financial inclusion of poor people, especially those in more remote and rural areas that formal financial institutions, even microfinance institutions, have found difficult to reach. The SG model involves a limited period of training input to promote a simple group-based methodology to collect savings from and lend to members. The potential for reaching more remote, more rural, and poorer populations stems from the basic parameters of the methodology, which can be adapted to local contexts. Since members own and manage their groups, they neither pay to support an external service provider nor incur the cost of external capital.

   This chapter examines the extent to which SG programmes are in fact tackling the frontiers of financial inclusion to reach remote, poor, and marginalized people, by profiling the areas and people that are reached by the methodology. We review the experiences of programmes seeking to reach particular marginalized and vulnerable groups such as young people, orphans and vulnerable children, and those living with HIV/AIDS. Some of the experiences in the evolution of the savings group methodology are reviewed, indicating issues that have arisen in replicating the model, and showing that once engaged, target groups often adjust the methodology to better suit their needs in ways that are not always in accordance with the 'rules'. The chapter concludes with a summary of findings and questions for further research.

Who are the members of savings groups?

Targeting strategies

With its evolution from the Mata Masu Dubara (MMD) programme in Niger, the SG model NGOs typically promote has a focus on rural areas. Extending their programmes to places such as Zanzibar, Uganda, and Mali, NGOs have targeted remote and isolated parts of countries where the population is far from paved roads, secondary schools and higher education, and major health facilities. A minority of people in these locations have access to electricity or clean water. Programmes also tend to be isolated from major market centres including regional and national markets (Allen, 2002; BARA and IPA, 2010; CARE, 2011; EMC and Wancer, n.d.).

In order to target such areas, organizations first use national and regional socioeconomic data and consult with a range of stakeholders and key informants to find the locations most in need of services. Additionally, organizations may use local-level techniques such as community mapping with community-based organizations (CBOs) and local authorities to identify the poorest and most marginalized populations (CARE, 2011).

When such communities have been identified, the organizations – often including local partners of international NGOs – hold meetings to explain the programme, invite people to form groups, and discuss the criteria that people should use to select their fellow members. For example, one SG model involves self-selection on characteristics such as honesty, punctuality, ability to save, and position within the community. The result is that members tend to select fellow participants with a similar social status (Vanmeenen, 2010).

While self-selection is the dominant organizing approach, Rwanda offers an example of more specific targeting. In order to ensure outreach to extremely poor people, one programme used government data to select districts, consulted district officials to identify villages with the highest concentrations of poverty, and finally asked village leaders to help identify the most vulnerable and trustworthy potential members to join. The programme's vulnerability criteria included marginalization, disability, living with AIDS or orphans, and widowhood. Potential members were then invited to a meeting, during which a poverty-profiling tool was used to ensure that the criteria had been met. In the scaling-up stage, village agents who were members of trained

---

Box 2.1 Targeting vulnerable groups in Rwanda

Judith Nyirantarama, aged 51, is married with seven children. Her husband left her in 2002, so she raises her children alone. Due to poverty and starvation, five of the children have left to become street children, commonly known as 'mayibobo'. Judith became a beggar in the village market in 2001. In December 2009, Judith was selected by her community members to join an SG group in Gacaca sector, Kabilizi Cell, and Mata Village called TWITEZIMBERE. She is now an active member of the group and is able to pay for her weekly shares. More importantly, she is a model for loan use in her group. She used her first loan of 3,000 RWF (about $5) to sell tomatoes and small fish. She has since taken more loans and expanded her business to include bananas and other vegetables. Her business is progressing well and she plans to expand it even further. Her living conditions have improved tremendously. Her five children are now back home, and she is able to provide meals and clothes for her whole family. She has also bought three rabbits, a sheep, a radio, and medical insurance commonly known as 'mutuelle de santé' for herself and all her seven children.

Source: Umoh and Bakliwal, 2011: 7

groups recruited new members and applied similar criteria. This approach ensured that the poorest were reached, and were slightly better represented in the groups than among non-members (Umoh and Bakliwal, 2011).

However, organizations such as the Aga Khan Foundation (AKF), Catholic Relief Services (CRS), Oxfam, and Plan International have also adopted a strategy in which they seek to saturate the chosen geographic areas with SGs to ensure that all those who are interested can join (CARE, 2011; BARA, 2008). For instance, after having identified the areas with the lowest socioeconomic indicators, Plan aims to reach every community within a district or cluster of districts from the areas identified (CARE, 2011). In one organization's methodology, the 'conception of replication and saturation derives from the assumption that if most eligible villagers are members, the poorest people in a village will also have been reached' (BARA, 2008).

The context of savings groups

Because SG programmes have been predominantly located in rural areas, agriculture is a dominant livelihood activity for members. In programme communities in Guatemala, for example, primary sources of income include agricultural day labour, subsistence agriculture, and trade of agricultural products and animals. Such work is largely subsistence-based, and its output is mainly for home consumption (Kaminaga et al., 2011). In one programme area in Tanzania, 87 per cent of the population is engaged in the agricultural sector, and 66 per cent of GDP is earned through agriculture, while only 27 per cent comes from other natural resources, five per cent from livestock, and less than three per cent from industry and other sectors (AKF, 2011).

The natural resource base of such income sources leads to seasonality and vulnerability. In a programme area in Cambodia, only 23 per cent of members earned an income that could be defined as consistent throughout the year (EMC and Wancer, n.d.). Of course, poor people living in rural areas try to compensate for the seasonality and vulnerability of their incomes through livelihood diversification. Other income-generating activities (IGAs) in Guatemala included the production and sale of handicrafts, salaried work, and small-scale commerce (Kaminaga et al., 2011). In Kenya and Uganda, trading and small businesses were the main additional activities, with only a few having formal jobs, or domestic or farm employment in better-off houses (Beijuka and Odele, 2007; Odera and Muruka, 2007). In three remote and mountainous regions of Tajikistan, women in member households were housewives (36 per cent) and some were government employees (12 per cent). Men in SG households were primarily engaged in government work (21 per cent), casual work (13 per cent), studying (11 per cent), and farming (10 per cent). In Tajikistan, the main sources of total cash income per household were salary (41 per cent), trading (18 per cent), and remittances (12 per cent) (AKF, 2009). In these areas, tree and livestock ownership are particularly important. Trees provide food, fuel for heating and cooking, and construction material;

95 per cent of households interviewed owned trees, and 81 per cent had livestock (AKF, 2009).

Most studies show that households have more than one source of income, both among those with current SG members and those in areas where programmes were being started. In Cambodia, for example, households tended to have two or more livelihood activities. The main livelihood activities in an area to which the SG programme is expanding are rice farming (63 per cent), raising livestock (26 per cent), agricultural labour (21 per cent), vegetable and fruit farming (13 per cent), and food or drink stands (10 per cent) (EMC and Wancer, n.d.). In Zanzibar, a study found that both existing members and incoming members had more than one income generating activity; the slightly higher number of activities members had could itself be a result of belonging to the SGs (Brannen, 2010).

In villages in the Segou Region of Mali to which an SG programme was expanding, a third of women were involved in agricultural activities, while about half of them were also involved in at least one business activity – usually petty trading. However, these activities were often linked to agriculture, and therefore subject to seasonality and vulnerable to shocks. More than half the villages in this area have experienced flooding or drought in the last five years. More than half the households participating in the study experienced at least one shock in the preceding 12 months that had negative economic conse-quences on their well-being. The most common negative events for these households were poor harvests due to drought, illness or injury of a member of the immediate household, illness or theft of animals, and poor harvest due to flooding (BARA and IPA, 2010). In another part of Mali where SGs have been introduced, the population consisted of nomads, agro-pastoralists, gold mining families (which required women to be away from home for long periods of time, sometimes all or part of the year), and seasonal migrants forced out by the dry season. In this context, migrating women had developed strategies to retain their involvement, including:

- coordination among group members who migrate to the same place in order to maintain their meetings and stay in contact with their trainer via mobile phone;
- leaving the savings deposit with relatives in the village to pay to the group in their absence;
- reimbursing the amount they owe in savings deposits to group funds for the number of weeks that they missed once they returned to the village; and
- sending their savings back home to contacts in the village for an on-time payment (Deubel and Nowak, 2012).

In a new programme area in Cambodia, almost 70 per cent of baseline participants experienced a negative event in the 12 months preceding the study, and on average, each household experienced more than one such event. The main shock was the illness or injury of one member of the household, experienced by 48 per cent of the participants. Illness or death of livestock and harvest failure or crop loss were the other most common negative events, and were similarly experienced by existing members (EMC and Wancer, n.d.). In South Africa, on the other hand, an SG programme is working in poor and remote areas but with a large proportion of women who are dependent on state transfers (see Box 2.2).

Research has shown that rural populations being targeted by SG programmes have little access to formal financial services, so informal financial services dominate use. Only 13 per cent of the women interviewed in Guatemala for a baseline said that they or a member of their household had saved or deposited money within the past year, while 20 per cent had taken a loan (Kaminaga et al., 2011). Over half of these loans (57 per cent) were taken from formal banks; only five per cent were taken through an MFI. In two Kenyan provinces where SGs are operating, exclusion from formal services was higher than for Kenya's rural population. However, use of informal services – mainly ROSCAs and ASCAs – was in fact slightly higher than for rural Kenya as a whole, suggesting the relative familiarity with informal group-based systems in these areas (DAI, 2010). In Zanzibar, almost half of mature SG members were saving before joining a savings group, while only about eight per cent of them had had access to loans (Brannen, 2010).

In Mali, the availability of both formal and informal financial services in one new programme area is very low, with about a quarter of the villages

---

Box 2.2 Savings groups in rural areas of South Africa

SaveAct is a South African NGO that builds on an existing savings culture by training mainly women and youth in poor rural areas to form savings groups, become financially literate, and develop enterprise opportunities. SaveAct has been active since 2006 in two of South Africa's poorest provinces: first Kwazulu-Natal (KZN), and subsequently the Eastern Cape (EC). According to provincial data, in 2005, half the population in KZN lived in poverty, and 12 per cent lived on less than $1 per day. Piloted in 2006, the SaveAct programme now reaches 850 groups with over 20,000 total members, some 90 per cent of whom are women. SaveAct also serves some peri-urban areas where inhabitants have slightly better access to water and electricity than the rural average. Baseline data for incoming members in KZN shows that over half of members were over 40 years old, with only 20 per cent under 30; most lived in a household with an average of seven members. Compared to a provincial literacy rate of 89 per cent and a national female literacy rate of 87 per cent in 2007 (World Bank, 2007), about 60 per cent of group participants felt able to write and read a letter. Incomes in the area were more dependent on state benefits and employment than in other African countries. Members' major income sources were: child grants (75 per cent); employment, including casual work (59 per cent); state pensions (47 per cent); and disability grants (22 per cent). Most members reported receiving their transfer payments through paypoints, and few used formal financial institutions. Accordingly, SGs scheduled their meetings so that members could draw from their transfers to save. Before joining SGs, the majority of participants were saving through *stokvels* (78 per cent) and burial societies (69 per cent),[1] while only 26 per cent were using a formal bank and almost none were using an MFI.

Source: Van der Riet, 2009

having an MFI or bank available in the area, and just seven per cent of villages having an MFI located in the village itself (CARE, 2011). The 35 per cent of women who had taken at least one loan during the preceding 12 months had mainly borrowed from relatives, friends, or neighbours, showing that 'nominal accessibility often translates to the de facto exclusion of women when travel is required' (BARA and IPA, 2010: 56). About 40 per cent of villages in a programme expansion area in Mali have one *tontine* (ROSCA), while some 25 per cent of them have more than one. Women in this area are not new to *tontines*: 42 per cent of respondents have participated in a *tontine* at some point in their lives, while about 19 per cent of the participants were current members of one at the time of the study (BARA and IPA, 2010). More than 40 per cent of women were also saving outside *tontines* – 39 per cent at home (BARA and IPA, 2010), but less than 1.5 per cent through a bank, cooperative, NGO, savings and loan association, or labour association (CARE, 2011). Thus, for women, both borrowing and saving tended to involve networks of friends and relatives rather than formal institutions (BARA and IPA, 2010). Evidence suggests that SGs were accessible to those unable to commit to *tontines* because of their smaller weekly contribution, but some 21 per cent of members were participating in *tontines* also, and they tended to form SGs with their fellow *tontine* members.

Gender, age, marital status, education, and empowerment

SG programmes have a predominantly female membership. According to the SAVIX database, the mean proportion of women in the 130 programmes reporting in September 2011 was 82 per cent. This compares to a mean of 78 per cent across the 1,176 institutions reporting to the MIX Market microfinance database in 2010.[2] The concentration of women in SGs can be explained in part by explicit targeting strategies adopted by organizations to reverse women's exclusion from financial services. In Ethiopia and Nepal, some programmes are working exclusively with women (Abebe and H/selassie, 2009; Valley Research Group and Mayoux, 2008) while in Kenya and Uganda, some are targeting the 'economically active poor, especially women' (Beijuka and Odele, 2007; Odera and Muruka, 2007). One programme noted an increase in the number of men joining SGs (Odera and Muruka, 2007), from five per cent in 2007 to 17 per cent in 2011, which is likely due to the group's expansion beyond its initial focus on OVC caretakers who were mainly women (SAVIX, 2012).[3]

According to some practitioners, savings groups programmes target women because they are often the ones in charge of the well-being of their household and children (CARE, 2011). However, a study conducted in Cambodia shows that the majority of SG members are women because, as per traditional gender roles, women typically manage the household's savings (EMC and Wancer, n.d.). Another study in Swaziland suggests that men are in the minority even when organizations are not targeting women exclusively because the amount of money saved and borrowed in a savings group is too little to be of any interest to them. Additionally, in some cultures it is considered shameful for a man to publicly show that he is not able to take care of his household (Zollmann, 2010).

Studies suggest that the majority of group members are between 30 and 50 years old, with the average usually in the high 30s. The average age of members in Ethiopia was 37, with almost 32 per cent of members aged 21–30 and 38 per cent aged 31–40. In Cambodia, average member age was 38. In Kenya, where the average age for adults was 40[4], 52 per cent of women and 72 per cent of men were over 40; but only 13 per cent of women and eight per cent of men were under 30 (DAI, 2010). Evidence for members in the Zanzibar programme, which had been left some years earlier, suggests that the average age of entry into the programme was 33, both for existing and incoming members (Brannen, 2010). This evidence suggests that, similar to those participating in many microfinance programmes, SG members are relatively mature in years; for example, the average ages of members across three microfinance programmes was between 38 and 43 (Sewa, India; ACP/Mibanco, Peru; and Zambuko Trust, Zimbabwe) (Cohen and Snodgrass, 2002).

Members are also usually married; their household sizes are likely to reflect the average, consistent with both the rural focus and with their members' average age. A study in Kenya found that the average size of SG members' households was six members, while the average household size in Kenya is 5.5 members (DAI, 2010). However, when savings groups are reaching particular marginalized groups, the households can be even bigger. Again in Kenya, where an SG programme was combined with an HIV and OVC programme, the average size of households was between eight and 10 members (Odera and Muruka, 2007).

A study in Mali shows that the large majority of women in the programme area lived in complex households where they shared meals, food storage, and other activities, often with other wives. They were typically married with children and between 20 and 49 years of age. Their decision-making abilities within the household differed depending on the type of decision involved. Nevertheless, less than half of them stated that their ability to make decisions in the households was high with respect to food, school and health expenses for their children, personal health, and visits to friends in the village. However, 58 per cent of them reported that they had a high level of decision-making ability with respect to their business activity (BARA and IPA, 2010).

In one region of Tajikistan, household decisions were clearly dominated by men, and for all domains male decision-making exceeded female decision-making. Decisions related to family planning, health expenditure, and loan taking were more likely to be made jointly, while women's decision-making power was highest related to savings (28 per cent). In two other regions within Tajikistan, the situation was somewhat similar, with a few exceptions in which women's level of decision-making was actually higher than men's. For instance, in one region women were making decisions related to household spending more frequently than men, while in another region women were making decisions on education spending, weddings, and family planning more frequently than men (AKF, 2009). Data collected in Guatemala showed that members already tended to be more empowered than non-members when they joined the SG programme. In particular, there was a significant difference in the number of members who were more likely to be members of other social groups. Also, more members were likely to say that they could participate in groups as much as they wanted to and more likely reported that they could make decisions about their own health independently as well as decide to visit friends in neighbouring villages (Kaminaga et al., 2011).

Members' education varies by programme, but overall literacy rates are high, with the majority of members able to read and write (CARE, 2011). Of six programmes reviewed by CARE, three had female literacy rates 3–4 percentage points below the national average for women (Kenya, Lesotho, and Rwanda) while three had rates that were 10 or more percentage points above the national average (Malawi, Tanzania, and Zambia), with the national averages themselves varying from 41 per cent to 95 per cent. With a few exceptions, usually the literacy level of male members is higher than that of female members. In some cases SG programmes are directly linked with other developmental programmes aiming to increase the level of education of their members. One approach also offers literacy training, and data shows that the literacy rates among its members doubled due to the programme – from 16 per cent to 34 per cent (Abebe and H/selassie, 2009).

Poverty outreach

Indicators commonly used to assess the depth of outreach of microfinance programmes include average savings and loan balances outstanding, either relative to income per head in a country or in US dollar terms. Figures 2.1a and 2.1b present these data for MFI and SG programmes globally.[5]

First, the mean savings balances members hold with SGs is US$20, while for MFIs it is $282 (Figure 2.1a). Because of the SG methodology, fewer members are able to hold a loan at any one time: The average proportion of borrowers to members at any one time is 36 per cent in SGs compared to 97 per cent in MFIs, highlighting the credit-led methodology of MFIs. For borrowers, the average outstanding loan size in SGs was $28, compared to $493 for MFIs. Hence SG savings balances are on average seven per cent of the level of MFIs, and outstanding loans are six per cent of the MFI level. Since 75 per cent of SG programmes for which data is available are located in Africa, this comparison has been undertaken for Africa alone and gives a very similar picture.[6,7]

When depth of outreach is measured in relation to GNI per capita (Figure 2.1b), MFI and SG savings are 19 per cent and seven per cent, respectively, of GNI per capita, indicating that mean savings balances are much lower for SGs than for MFIs. Comparing MFI and SG borrowers with outstanding loans, the figures are 34 per cent and five per cent of GNI per capita respectively. The differences between SGs and MFIs in terms of the ratio to GNI per capita are

Figure 2.1 Comparison of MFI and SG average savings per member and oustanding loans per borrower

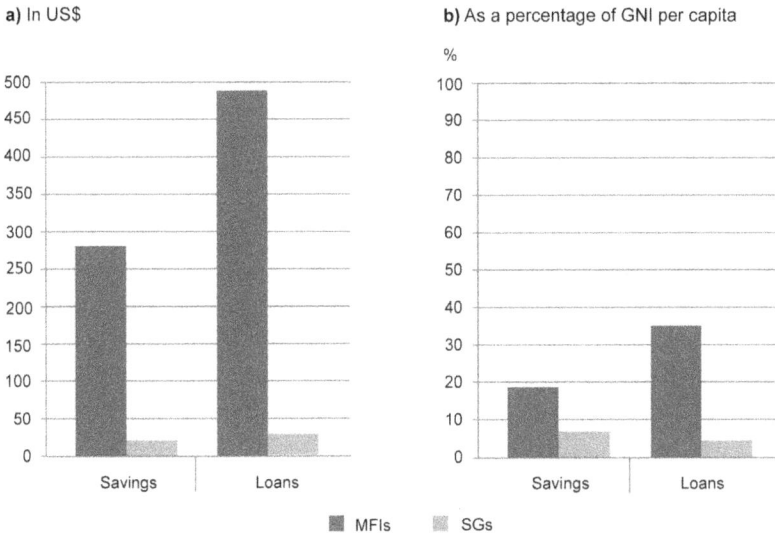

a) In US$

b) As a percentage of GNI per capita

■ MFIs   ▨ SGs

Source: MIX Market data for fiscal year 2010; SAVIX databases, data for September 2011

less severe for both savings and outstanding loans than the mean balances in US dollars because of the fact that many MFIs operate in countries with higher GNI per capita. When these figures are examined for Africa alone, the picture is even more favourable to SGs, with SG savings at one-fifth those of MFIs, and outstanding loans at one-twentieth. The comparison of saving and borrowing levels in SGs and MFIs suggests that SG outreach in Africa is particularly deep by comparison to MFIs.

As with other microfinance programmes, relatively few studies systematically collect data on poverty levels of members such that poverty outreach can be assessed. Some programmes are now using the Progress out of Poverty Index (PPI) to gather data which we review here to assess their depth of outreach. It is important to note that data has sometimes been collected in baselines and sometimes during active programme operation, in which case it may reflect improvements in status since members joined.

According to a study conducted in Cambodia, 13 per cent of members were likely to fall under the national poverty line and four per cent of members were likely to fall under the USAID Extreme Poverty Line, while non-members were more likely to do so with rates of 22 per cent and eight per cent respectively.[8] However, all these rates are lower than the 30 per cent of households living below the national poverty line, suggesting that the programmes are attracting the moderately poor and those on medium incomes rather than the poor or very poor, a suggestion also substantiated by data on assets, land ownership, government poverty rankings, and qualitative data (EMC and Wancer, n.d.).

In Ecuador, the placement of the SG programme was dependent on requests from communities, and when the study was undertaken, some 25 per cent of the (by then mature) SG members were found to be below the national poverty line according to the PPI (Fleischer Proaño et al., 2010), compared to 31 per cent of households below the national poverty line in 2009. This may in part arise from improvements to some members' status as a result of the programme.

In Guatemala on the other hand, where the rate of household poverty incidence is 40 per cent (2006) (World Bank, 2007), the programme targeted poorer areas of the country. A baseline survey using the PPI with both members and non-members showed that 67 per cent of new members were likely to be below the poverty line, compared to 72 per cent of non-members; 25 per cent of the whole sample was classified as 'very poor' (Kaminaga et al., 2011). This data suggests that it is possible to attract a much higher proportion of poor people than the average in areas where the overall poverty rate is higher. Even so, the higher poverty incidence among non-members was mainly a result of data on villages where the programme had not yet reached, and this may also reflect the fact that it is easier to start programmes in areas with relatively lower poverty incidence, even within poorer areas.

These results contrast significantly with findings from the baseline study in Mali for areas in which SGs were being newly promoted, where more than half of respondents fell below the $1.25 per day poverty line, and more than 90 per cent of respondents fell below the $2.50 per day poverty line (BARA and IPA, 2010), compared to national poverty rates of 48 per cent and 80 per cent at these poverty lines. Although it is not yet known whether the poverty profile of members actually joining will be biased upward, PPI data from a very small sample study (n=41) of members in Mali indicated that 74 per cent lived below the national poverty line, compared to a national figure of 48 per cent in 2005 (Miller and Gash, 2010), suggesting the programme tends to attract a higher proportion of poor people in this context.

The importance of targeting areas with higher levels of poverty is further emphasized by data from east Africa. In Kenya, some 64 per cent of members' households fell below the national poverty line, compared to a national household poverty rate of 38 per cent (Ferguson, 2012). The much higher poverty rate for members is ascribed to strong geographic targeting to some of the poorest areas of Kenya's coastal region. By contrast, in Uganda, where geographic targeting was not as strongly undertaken, the poverty rate of member households is lower than the national average (15 per cent compared to 19 per cent), but the difference is less dramatic. In Tanzania the rate was consistent with the national average at 27 per cent of households.

As indicated above, in Rwanda, targeting specifically sought to include marginalized and excluded groups; as a result, 63 per cent of members are below the national poverty line (2009) compared to 54 per cent nationally (2006 data) (Coulibaly, 2012).

There is little to suggest that groups specifically seek to exclude people with specific social, economic, or demographic backgrounds. The reality is simply that when encouraged to form groups of people who are honest and trustworthy, organizers are likely to approach those they know best, and most are likely to have similar characteristics. Early adopters tend to be those who are most able to take risks as a result not only of wealth but also better information and networks, while some people will opt out due to social exclusion or shame (BARA and IPA, 2010).

The Cambodia study also concluded that while there did not appear to be explicit processes of social exclusion from groups, the very poor were often perceived as unable to save, or as a credit risk. Often isolated both geographically and by low social and economic status, the very poor faced challenges in learning about and participating in promotional meetings. The tendency to form groups among social networks meant that it was difficult to form groups among either the 'very poor' or the 'rural rich' (EMC and Wancer, n.d.). In addition, the mandatory weekly savings with the group represents an obstacle for those who have unstable or irregular sources of income (BARA, 2008; EMC and Wancer, n.d.; Miller and Gash, 2010).

Research in Mali provides evidence that early joiners come from all levels of wealth in the village, and highlights that the risk-takers join first (Bermudez and Matuszeski, 2010). However, findings also point to processes through which the poorest women were left in the lowest quality groups – those formed through replication and often inadequately trained. Older women, often late adopters, struggled to understand the SG accounting practices. The replication methodology itself may induce the creation of groups of poorer quality for the poorest women (BARA, 2008).

Furthermore, there is evidence of segregation of minorities or those who are outliers for various reasons. A few groups were formed for first wives separately from second wives at the instigation of the animator, while artisanal castes who tended to live outside the village were left to form their own groups for logistical reasons. Concerns about dynamics of programme outreach to minority communities have also been found in relation to pastoralists and migrant communities in Mali. While some had adopted strategies for making their contributions in absentia – such as meeting in another location or leaving funds with relatives – language barriers impeded both communication with these minority groups and efforts to adapt the programme to their particular livelihood patterns (Deubel and Nowak, 2012).

Summary

This overview suggests that SGs are indeed providing savings and loan services in amounts that are much lower than mainstream MFIs. They target poor rural areas and reach mainly women who are over 30, married with children, and often able to have their own income sources. Their level of literacy is similar to or above the average for their country.

The data on poverty outreach suggests that where national poverty rates are lower – such as in Ecuador and Cambodia – the proportion of those below the poverty line included in an SG programme may be lower than the national average, even when rural areas are targeted. This in turn suggests that more deliberate targeting is useful to ensure poverty outreach where national poverty rates are lower. The Kenyan case demonstrates this well for geographic targeting, while the Rwandan case demonstrates the usefulness of orientation towards excluded groups. Where self-selection is the main recruitment mechanism and poverty rates are low, poorer people are less likely to be early adopters and more likely to be marginalized by the majority. Where poverty rates are high, poor people are more likely to be included as SGs form. Geographic targeting toward communities with relatively high poverty incidence is likely to make inclusion of poor people easier. Where poverty incidence is lower or inequality is greater, more specific targeting of the poor will likely be required to ensure their inclusion.

The evidence also raises questions as to whether the 'saturation' strategy will in fact reach particular poor and marginalized groups. It suggests that stronger targeting may be needed if vulnerable or marginalized social groups are to join SGs. The case of the Rwanda programme demonstrates that the application of criteria in recruitment, including vulnerability and marginalization, can better ensure that such groups are included, and suggests that facilitating agencies consider targeting strategies to achieve their inclusion objectives. Strategies that involve targeting of more specific vulnerable and excluded groups can allow for replication in a 'trickle up' manner as others see it working, whereas the vulnerable groups may perceive greater barriers to replicating the methodology (e.g. it is not for them) where replication is expected to 'trickle down'.

The focus on women is also an important issue for consideration. Women's exclusion from formal financial services is historically well-evidenced, and their high participation in SG programmes is an important contribution to improved financial inclusion. In rural contexts, however, men too are often excluded from both formal and informal financial services; the SG methodology has the potential to offer them a useful service. One male SG member commented in recent research in Kenya, 'Someone who makes little money like me cannot qualify for a bank loan' (Johnson et al., 2012: 26). Male-only groups have often been found to be difficult to work with in microfinance programmes, and in African contexts men are less likely to be familiar with informal group systems because norms of socialization do not operate for men as they do for women. In addition, men's capital requirements are often for larger sums, and more co-variant than women's (e.g. for agricultural inputs, school fees) so that multiple demands may be made on the group fund at the same time, potentially creating competition among members (Johnson, 2004). As a result, men may be more ambitious in setting contribution levels at the beginning and find it harder to continue with them. Adapting the methodology to better reach them presents a challenging objective if SGs are to substantially contribute to financial inclusion for both genders. Strategies are needed that will enable men to mobilize and form or find groups in which they can operate (which may be mixed groups); these strategies must facilitate both saving amounts of money that are useful to men as well as effective enforcement and sanctioning mechanisms.

Reaching young people and people affected by HIV/AIDS

Beyond the mainstream SG membership outlined in Section 2, 'Who are the members of savings groups', facilitating agencies have been particularly endeavouring to reach two social groups: young people (15–24 years of age) and those affected by HIV/AIDS. In the context of rapid population growth, the youth 'bulge' in developing countries represents both a challenge to facilitate their transition to economic independence, and an opportunity for financial services; by engaging youth with more systematized services, their future financial inclusion may be better secured. Similarly, with the majority of SG programmes operating in Africa – some 70 per cent of those that report to the SAVIX database – the importance of responding to the HIV/AIDS epidemic has also been a concern of promoters. This section reviews some developments in promoting SGs with these populations.

Reaching young people

Acknowledging the economic difficulties that poor young people are facing, especially in their transition to economic independence, a programme in Mali is introducing SGs to respond to young people's financial needs (FFH, 2011a; FFH and AIM Youth, n.d.). Market research found that young people face financial pressures related to key life events to which they are expected to contribute, such as marriage, childbirth (including for adolescent girls), and migration. To cope, they engage in a variety of income-generating activities; young women braid hair and make condiments; young men engage in casual and agricultural labour. Young men in particular are likely to migrate seasonally both to increase their own incomes and to support their families. From these income sources they are able to save very small amounts (e.g. $0.05 per week) and use informal methods to do so – usually by saving in their homes. However, typically they do not hold the funds for long, given family pressures and their own regular expenses for food or toiletries. Young people also reported borrowing from their parents, but worried about confidentiality and a bad image if they did not repay.

The Mali programme uses the standard SG methodology: young people form groups of 10–15 participants, and with the guidance of a field agent they learn group management. Most youth programmes also integrate financial education to help them to identify their goals, prioritize their spending, and systematically determine the amounts they can afford to borrow. These groups are also usually engaged in social objectives to tackle those issues affecting young people in the village; for example, they may decide to clean the village or plant trees in areas that have been heavily deforested. The groups can be single-sex or mixed and include married as well as unmarried members. As of June 2011, this programme reached 6,793 young people through 483 groups; 52 per cent of members were female. Seventy-seven per cent of members were between 13 and 17 years of age, while 21 per cent were between 18 and 24. Forty-four per cent were still in school, and 10 per cent were married. Young people's savings groups can also decide to have a godmother, an adult woman experienced in the Saving for Change (SfC) methodology who can provide guidance to the group.

Young people's mobility has emerged as an important challenge to the SG model. Young people are on the move – to find work, to marry, to seek other opportunities – resulting in uneven participation that challenges the success of the SG annual cycle (FFH, 2011a; FFH and AIM Youth, n.d.).

A programme targeting young people in Niger, Senegal, and Sierra Leone is also operating to integrate other activities into the groups (Plan International Canada, 2009; Winnebah, 2011). In taking the SG approach to young people, the methodology again involves stages of training during which the members gradually take over the management of the group. The programme also encourages the emergence of community volunteers from the groups who can be certificated and go on to train other groups on a fee-for-service basis. In addition, the programme includes further training to help youth develop successful businesses and facilitate their transition to adulthood. Training options vary in response to participant preferences and include literacy and numeracy, ICT training, and life skills – covering gender equality, human and child rights, health, and sexual education. In Niger and Senegal, over 80 per cent of the members are young women, whereas in Sierra Leone there are more young men, although young women are still in the majority (68 per cent). In Sierra Leone, the programme initially had a majority of young men until it adjusted its recruitment to encourage girls to participate. The young women are mainly unmarried, not in school, and have average ages of 19 to 21. They already participate in income-generating activities such as trade and domestic work, which give them irregular and vulnerable income streams. Their greatest challenge in meeting the regular saving requirement at the time of the study was the unreliability of their incomes, which they tried to overcome through saving on other items (usually food and snacks). In Senegal, members were using their SG loans to make investments in their businesses; in Sierra Leone members were using their savings mainly to meet unexpected needs, and their loans primarily for their businesses or education (FFH, 2011b).

Vulnerable adolescent girls dependent on transactional sex to meet their basic financial needs were targeted in Burundi by a programme covering savings, financial education, human rights, and sexual health. The 12,000 girls who joined these SGs were aged 14–22 and almost evenly divided between students and those out of school. The former often got the money for their weekly savings deposit from their parents, and ran income-generating activities during school vacations or with their mothers. The SG members no longer in school worked together as casual labourers to raise money for their group savings. These 'bad' girls, described as 'surly vagabonds', had largely been written off by their families and communities; many were stunned when the girls started income-generating activities with their own resources. Their success has motivated their brothers and other young men to start their own groups (Nelson and Butzberger, 2011).

Apart from these efforts to target young people, an interesting case of self-replication was found in Mali where a few groups of children, usually under 12–13 years of age, formed with the help of members of mature adult groups. The replicated groups were created at the request of one or more children, usually daughters of current members; almost all child members had someone in their family who was part of an adult savings group, usually the mother or grandmother. The children were saving for different purposes, and many of them were already operating a small business or helping in their mother's business. These groups were run in the same way as adult groups, with the same regulations and fines. Children contributed weekly savings which they received from their parents or grandparents. However, it was found that the children usually took loans to help their parents, although some were also using loans to pay for their education and the share-out monies to buy school uniforms. Since these groups have been created in an area where programme rules for adult SGs prohibit multiple memberships or multiple shares, parents may have viewed the formation of children's groups as a relatively safe way to save more and receive additional loans (Edwards, 2010). Nevertheless, this adaptation introduces children to savings at a young age and gives them opportunities to learn money management skills.

In Central America it was also found that women were keen to introduce savings to their children (CRS, 2011). An adapted SG programme combining savings and education was introduced because children, it was believed, would not be able to handle loans. Instead, they were taught the use of money and savings, their rights and responsibilities, and environmental protection.

These experiences raise a number of issues for SGs working with young adults and children.[9] First is the issue of whether and at what age a young person can balance enterprise and money management with other activities important to their development, including education and family responsibilities. Also important to examine is the extent to which younger children in particular may be seen as an additional conduit for resources by adults. A second major issue is how sustainability should be viewed for youth SGs; it may not be realistic to expect such groups to continue far into the future, as might be the case for their adult counterparts. Additionally, replication strategies among the youth population may be compromised by the likely shorter terms of trained replicators, given the changing life circumstances of young people. It may be more reasonable to view youth SGs as an educational experience that helps prepare young people to manage their finances.

Reaching people affected by HIV/AIDS

Targeting children and young people has also been an approach intended to help mitigate the impact of HIV on orphans and vulnerable children (OVC). In Zimbabwe, where there are approximately 1.7 million OVC[10], one programme targeted 13- to 24-year-olds both in and out of school to meet their financial needs and improve their overall well-being. The SG methodology was introduced to 3,600 participants meeting regularly in school classrooms for savings activities along with additional training on health issues, life skills, and child rights; participants could also request specific training according to their interests (CARE, 2011).

Since 2005, a programme in Rwanda targeted to OVC and child-headed households (CHH – defined as those between 13 and 18 years old), has attempted to meet some of the financial and psychological needs of these youth. Since the goal was to help OVC households in building financial assets through access to safe financial services and education, the programme needed to combine SGs with vocational and business skills training. The SG methodology did not need any particular adaptation for this context, although the groups comprised both adults and young people and sometimes young people alone (Dills et al., 2009; Mukankusi et al., 2009).

In Kenya, SGs were also introduced within existing programmes supporting orphans and those affected by HIV/AIDS by providing home-based care, medicines, uniforms, and books. Participation in SGs allows members to build lump sums, access emergency funds, and use credit to diversify their income sources and better cope with household shocks. These groups mainly reached women (95 per cent) although not all OVC and HIV programme participants have joined (Odera and Muruka, 2007).

In Tanzania, an SG programme combines literacy, community banking, and small business development along with information on issues such as HIV/AIDS, child care and protection, and gender-based and domestic violence. The

---

Box 2.3 A young member of an OVC programme in Rwanda

Alexis Habimana is a 16-year-old Rwandan boy who was left to care for his mother, six siblings, and two cousins after the passing of his father. In order to provide for his family, Alexis dropped out of school after completing only six years of education and joined a professional training programme that taught him carpentry skills. Within six months he had learned the basics of the trade, and then completed a two-month internship in a proper work environment.

Equipped with his new skills, Alexis is now earning more than $52 a month, a dramatic improvement from the $8 a month he previously earned. He is now able to provide food for his family and save approximately $2 a month through his local Savings and Internal Lending Community (SILC) group. He knows this is still only a small amount, but he hopes that in a year or so he will have saved enough to purchase more tools for his business. With a few more tools, Alexis knows that he can expand his services and increase the profit he brings home for his family.

Source: Mukankusi et al., 2009

programme aimed to give women caregivers of OVC opportunities to diversify and increase their income, and hence meet the needs of the children. By the end of 2008, 260 SGs with a total of 5,800 caregivers were functioning, prompting the introduction of the SG methodology to two major OVC programmes covering 46 districts of Tanzania. A total of 2,754 groups have been formed with 57,545 caregivers, who collectively care for 83,053 orphans and vulnerable children (Victoria Munene, personal communication, 2011).

When HIV prevalence rates in Zimbabwe were running at 25 per cent of the adult population around the year 2000, one SG project sought to reduce economic vulnerability and promote economic development within affected communities. Working in partnership with local AIDS Service Organizations (ASOs), the programme targeted five categories of people: widows, OVC, sex workers, care providers, and people living with HIV/AIDS. It had two components: the formation of SGs and the promotion of income-generating activities, including training in business literacy and practices. Much of the programme's success appears to have resulted from the training given in selection, planning, and management of businesses alongside the financial services themselves (Hendricks and Jain, 2005).

Operating in the poorest part of Tanzania where 68 per cent of people live below the basic-needs poverty line, a Mission Hospital HIV Project combined SGs and microenterprise development training with HIV awareness, voluntary counselling and testing (VCT), and compassionate home-based care for those living with HIV. This initiative was a response to an earlier failure of grants to jumpstart businesses among these groups. The possibility for groups to decide their internal rules gave them the freedom to choose their savings amount and meeting frequency, thus meeting their ability and matching their needs. The creation of a social fund also was identified as a strategy for members to cater to the needs of others, especially for the sick in their communities. Some groups even operated more than one fund in order to target different needs (e.g. one fund was used for the group and another for supporting orphans and widows) (Parrot, 2008).

Summary

The notable feature of all of the SG programmes that are reaching out to vulnerable and marginalized groups is their additional components beyond the promotion of the standard SG methodology. For young people, these add-ons are likely to be financial education, life skills, and other vocational and skills training, alongside social activities that build group identity and cohesion. Among people affected by HIV, skill development or business training are needed, as well as financial education for support and advice on financial management. Moreover, reaching people affected by HIV usually involves partnerships with organizations and programmes that have the skills and experience needed to provide caring social and medical support; the SG methodology must accommodate these key components.

Adapting the SG methodology for outreach

Experience demonstrates that the SG model can be attractive to a range of target groups because of its relative simplicity and accessibility. However, facilitating agencies are likely to need to adapt the model to context; indeed, members may do this themselves. This section reviews some experiences with adjusting SG methodologies to suit local needs, initiated both by facilitating NGOs and members. The section highlights issues facilitating agencies need to be aware of as they replicate the SG model in new contexts.

The intention of the SG methodology is to offer very simple financial inter-mediation by ensuring that the mechanism can be run by group members themselves with little (if any) ongoing external support. At the heart of tailoring the approach to new people and contexts is the balance between providing useful products – as determined by savings and loan amounts, contribution frequency, loan access, and repayment schedules – and achieving transparency and accountability in the operation of the mechanism. Greater product variety leads to more management complexity, which can in turn result in less accountability and transparency. Accountability and trans-parency can also be compromised when power and gender dynamics among members create opportunities for leaders or other influential people in the group to use the funds to their own advantage, with the eventual likelihood of group collapse (Johnson and Sharma, 2007).

Gender

As discussed above, SG programmes involve mainly women, but few are now entirely made up of women. In some of the early programmes, when men were involved in the groups, they tended to take on the role of bookkeeper as they were usually literate and women were not. However, men often did not comply well with the methodology, and could create repayment problems. As a result, in order to enable the women to manage the system alone, an oral bookkeeping system was created, with amounts recalled at each meeting by the members (BARA and IPA, 2010). Similar problems in Ghana also led members to begin keeping records visually, in order to avoid putting men in positions of power in the group. In Uganda, mixed groups caused some women to leave, as they thought that the resources of the group and the savings had been 'hijacked' by male members (Allen, 2002: 48). While many programmes now operate with mixed groups, with men usually in the minority, issues of gender dynamics are important and can affect SG operation.

The nature of intra-household relations can also influence how programmes are designed and promoted. In some instances, programmes have found it important to involve men in initial meetings promoting the approach in order to gain their approval (Allen, 2002); in Ethiopia, husbands initially challenged the all-women programme, but eventually they came to appreciate its value (Abebe and H/selassie, 2009). In Cambodia, loan applications have to be heard from the spouse (wife or husband) or someone else in the family; a good relationship with the village chief is also important (Seng et al., 2007). In Mali it was found that group failure was often due to a lack of support from husbands and village chiefs, and that men were often present in some way around the group activities: male 'observers' attended the meetings, and women needed to negotiate with their husbands on decision-making over their activities (Edwards, 2010). On the other hand, in Kenya, some SG members reported a positive impact of having couples as members – when the husband can understand his wife's role in the group, he is less likely to 'bother' her about it.[11]

Recordkeeping, shares, loans, interest, and share-outs

Recordkeeping is an area in which a number of approaches have been tried in order to achieve transparency and accountability for those with low levels of literacy. As indicated above, an oral recordkeeping system was chosen in Niger and Mali due to the low levels of literacy among women members. With time, other recordkeeping methodologies have been added, including written systems and a double system which uses elements of both oral and written methodology (although in Mali, the written component is largely symbolic). In Zanzibar and Uganda, for instance, members are using a written system with passbooks in which the amount of the shares bought are stamped with a symbol to allow easy tally of the total savings held (Allen, 2002). However, according to research conducted in Kenya, SG members have been reluctant to switch to the passbook methodology, preferring to keep the ledger system already in use. At the same time, some members prefer to keep their passbooks at home, and some groups are now using both systems (DAI, 2010). Given the low level of literacy and the high number of languages spoken in some areas, a passbook system can also be more user-friendly, while ledgers can be difficult to understand both for those keeping them as well as for others who might wish to review them.

While the original Niger model involved a fixed single share amount to be bought at each meeting, approaches have evolved to accommodate diverse capacities to save due to mixed wealth levels and the vagaries of income flows, by allowing variations in the number of shares bought at each meeting. In these cases, a group establishes the value of a single share and allows members to purchase between one and five shares at each meeting. The greater flexibility of multiple share purchases requires written records and also leads to more complex calculations at share-out. Where groups have only oral recordkeeping everyone must commit to purchase a fixed number of shares for the duration of the cycle.

Accommodating diverse capacities to save then involves either multiple memberships in the same or different groups. This may also be achieved by having a child or family member join the group to save for them. This allows the group to retain simple recordkeeping in which all 'members' have equal share holdings (Allen, 2002; BARA and IPA, 2010). Allowing multiple shares to be bought at each meeting is more flexible, but requires written records and increases the complexity of determining loan eligibility and share-outs. Such increased complexity can lead to the need for more member training, as was the case in Zanzibar where there were multiple shares, no regular fixed savings, and variable loan terms (Allen, 2002).

Moreover, setting the basic value of the share and the maximum number that can be purchased (usually five) is an issue that programmes and SG members have to consider carefully. These standards will affect the diversity of the members in the group and size of the loans they can take out. Hence, the greater the diversity of contributions allowed raises the potential for more heterogeneous membership, which may in turn lead to tensions. Setting the share price too high may exclude poorer people if everyone is required to save at each meeting. The challenge is to keep the workings of the group as simple as possible to ensure that the poorest and least educated can participate. One of the causes of exclusion identified in Cambodia, for example, was that members have difficulty in understanding the SG system (EMC and Wancer, n.d.).

Interest rates also require adaptation to context. Members agree on the interest rate they charge themselves; within the same area, group policies may differ. Some years after the programme in Zanzibar had been left by the promoter, it was found that 40 per cent of the groups visited had reduced the rate from five per cent to between one and three per cent (Anyango et al., 2007), while one group had decided not to charge interest at all, citing a conflict with Islamic laws. In Ecuador, groups tended to reduce the rate from the recommended 10 per cent to five per cent (Fleischer Proaño et al., 2010).

The issue of interest in Islamic contexts has been found to require particular sensitivity. In a conservative Islamic district in Mali, two groups were shut down as a result of charging interest which was not approved by husbands or the village chiefs (Edwards, 2010). Trying to reach Muslim communities in one Indian context, an organization contacted the Imams from the outset to secure their help in promoting the programme, and as a result, the interest charges were accepted when the methodology was explained. In another instance in Afghanistan, interest was initially a problem when the programme was first introduced, and no one was willing to get involved. The promoters decided to delay the discussion until sufficient funds had accumulated for lending, at which point they asked what appropriate charges for the funds would be; members agreed to pay 50 per cent of their earnings from the use of the funds. In another context, groups initially refused to charge any interest, but members were unhappy that they received no dividend, and the promoters found it necessary to carefully discuss with the group the consequences of their choices.[12]

The complexity of calculating the share-out directly results from the degree of variability in the share contribution system. Where the system involves a compulsory fixed share contribution by all members at each meeting, the share-out involves the equal division of the fund among the members at the end of the cycle – or on the basis of the total number of memberships where these are allowed. Variable share contributions result in more complex calculations since the share-out is intended to distribute the profits proportional to shares. In Kenya, studies have found that after the groups were left to conduct the share-outs themselves, the proportional approach that had been promoted was not the only one in evidence (Malkamaki, 2010; Odell and Rippey, 2010). Most commonly, members divided the fund equally among all, either because they found the proportional calculation too difficult to undertake or because they simply viewed this method as fair and as a means of supporting poorer members of the group. A further variation was simply to give the interest back to the member who had paid it, an approach also found in Swaziland. In this case, members felt that paying the interest back encouraged members to take loans (Zollman, 2010).

It is likely that savings groups will make adjustments to many aspects of the methodology in order to better fit their cash flows, needs for services, social characteristics, and cultural context. It is also to be expected that groups will deviate from the 'rules' as originally set out in the constitution as they do so. Adaptations to methodologies are in principle to be applauded, if they enable needs for financial services to be more effectively met. The critical issue with all adaptations – whether by facilitating agencies or groups – is twofold. First is the extent to which they create complexity that compromises members' ability to understand the system and hold leaders accountable; and, second, is the extent to which they offer opportunities for some members to benefit from group resources at the expense of other members. The extent to which loan multiples are increased, or loan terms are extended, or on-time repayment are not adequately enforced, will inevitably result in reduced circulation of funds and the potential stagnation and collapse of the mechanism. Adapting the methodology to the needs of members therefore involves supporting a judicious balance of these criteria at the outset, although with no guarantee that they will be retained over time.

Conclusion

This overview shows that SG programmes have concentrated on reaching rural areas; by intermediating much smaller savings balances into small-scale loans, SGs offer more prospects for the inclusion of poorer people than most forms of formal and semi-formal financial services can. However, by using self-selection as the main recruitment strategy in these areas, programmes tend to attract members who are relatively mature and established in their households. The evidence on poverty outreach raises very similar issues to that of the uptake of more mainstream microfinance programmes, and suggests that if reaching those below the poverty line is an important goal of SG programmes (rather than just reaching the financially excluded), SGs may require some targeting mechanism. Strategies that involve 'trickle up' of the methodology through saturation might work better in this respect than those that are left to 'trickle down'.

Moreover, even where targeting may not be specifically focused on women, the evidence shows that take-up of these programmes by women is greater than for men. While women do tend to face greater barriers to inclusion via the formal sector than men, the implication is that this is a methodology that better serves the needs of women than men. However, many poor men are also excluded from formal services. Hence, the potential of SGs to assist men is a topic that deserves further attention.

The evidence from programmes reaching young people and those affected by HIV/AIDS suggests that such projects are best integrated with other interventions. A similar approach is also being used with those internally displaced and living in refugee camps. At a minimum, financial education or training and business skills programmes are likely to be necessary for many marginalized groups, even where other needs of these groups are being met by parallel interventions.

This overview also shows that SG methodologies have been adjusted both by promoters and members to make them appropriate for their context. However, as the parameters of a group are changed to grant members more flexibility in saving and taking out loans, recordkeeping can become more complex, potentially compromising transparency and accountability. The risk is that greater complexity offers either greater scope for mistakes, or for more powerful members to exploit opportunities to manipulate the system in their favour. Programmes have made great efforts to strike an appropriate balance between flexibility and simplicity to avoid such problems.

Other issues for further research include the following:

- Data on poverty outreach is still limited, and while a few major studies will shed more light on this topic in the coming few years, it will also be necessary for SG promoters to collect more systematic data in order to offer evidence of poverty outreach.
- There is very limited evidence on how and to what extent programmes reach groups that are marginalized because of social differences such as religion, caste, and ethnicity. Research on effective strategies to reach these groups would therefore be of great value.
- Little evidence exists on the performance of programmes after promoters have left. How members' adaptations to the model and to the dynamics of their internal social structure contribute to better or worse performance is little understood.
- Action research might be undertaken on how to involve more men in SGs since the uptake is stronger among women, particularly in Africa. This disparity may be due to both gender dynamics in groups (men find it harder to form groups) and the amounts of money managed (men may need larger lump sums than women do, and therefore find that SGs do not tend to meet their needs). Strategies to address both of these issues need to be piloted.

Acknowledgements

The authors are grateful to comments on earlier versions received from marc bavois, Eloisa Devietti, Laura Fleischer, Megan Gash, Lauren Hendricks, Anton Krone, Janina Matuszeski, Victoria Munene, Candace Nelson, Katherine Oglietti, David Panetta, John Schiller, Guy Vanmeenen, and Kathy Younker. Errors of omission or commission remain their own.

Notes

1. *Stokvel* is the South African term for a ROSCA, and burial societies operate to provide funds and social support to members when a person dies.
2. Own calculation using Mix Market data for institutions reporting to the Mix in 2010. Retrieved from: www.mixmarket.org
3. Data derived from SAVIX database at www.savix.org [accessed 30 March 2012].
4. Original computation using FinAccess 2009.
5. Data on SGs is taken from the online SAVIX database at www.savix.org, and data on MFIs is taken from the MIX Market database at www.mixmarket.org. The data is global unless otherwise stated. Mean averages for each programme are weighted by programme size in terms of number of members.
6. Note that the ratios between these are not the same as those between the figures given as a percent of GNI per capita because of the very different levels of GNI per capita that exist across countries in which the different institutions operate. Both databases use PPP exchange rates.
7. Because some 70 per cent of SG programmes are in Africa, it is useful to separate Africa out from the global picture because we might expect these figures for MFIs to be lower than the global averages. However, the average MFI savings balance in Africa is lower at US$214, but the average outstanding loan balance is higher at $567.
8. Note that the PPI methodology is based on households in poverty rather than individuals. All national rates used here for comparative purposes are therefore of household poverty rates, i.e. the proportion of households living in poverty. These are usually lower than headcount national poverty rates. Additionally all household poverty rates are taken from PPI documentation for the country in question available at www.progressoutofpoverty.org.
9. We are particularly grateful to John Schiller for these points.
10. Figure cited by source as being from the 2005 National Action Plan for Orphans and Vulnerable Children.
11. Candace Nelson (2012), personal communication.
12. These points were made by participants in a workshop at the Arusha Savings Group Summit, October 2011.

References

Abebe, S. and H/selassie, B. (2009) 'Report on impact evaluation of WORTH literacy-led saving and credit program', Pact Ethiopia, Addis Ababa.

Aga Khan Foundation (AKF) (2009) 'Improving rural income through Community-Based Savings Groups (IRIS): Baseline study 2009', unpublished.

AKF (2011) 'Coastal Rural Support Programme, Tanzania CRSP (T): Project implementation plan agriculture and market development component 2010–2014', unpublished.

Allen, H. (2002) 'CARE International's Village Savings & Loan Programmes in Africa: Micro finance for the rural poor that works'. Retrieved from: <https://www.msu.edu/unit/phl/devconference/CAREVillSavLoanAfr.pdf>.

Anyango, E., Esipisu, E., Opoku, L., Johnson, S., Malkamaki, M., and Musoke, C. (2007) 'Village savings and loan associations: Experience from Zanzibar', *Small Enterprise Development* 18(1):11–24.

Beijuka, J. and Odele, S. (2007) 'Savings and Internal Lending Communities (SILC) in Uganda: Program review'. Retrieved from: <www.microsave.org/research_paper/savings-and-internal-lending-communities-silc-in-uganda>

Bermudez, L. and Matuszeski, J. (2010) 'Ensuring continued success: Saving for Change in older program areas of Mali', Oxfam America, Boston, MA.

Brannen, C. (2010) 'An impact study of the village savings and loan association (VSLA) program in Zanzibar, Tanzania', honors thesis, Wesleyan University. Retrieved from: <http://wesscholar.wesleyan.edu/etd_hon_theses/462>

Bureau of Applied Research in Anthropology (BARA) (2008) *Operational Evaluation of Saving for Change in Mali*, University of Arizona. Retrieved from: <http://savings-revolution.org/doclib/>

BARA and Innovations for Poverty Action (IPA) (2010) 'Baseline study of Saving for Change in Mali: Results from the Segou Expansion Zone and existing SfC Sites', BARA and IPA. Retrieved from: <www.ffhtechnical.org/resources/articles/baseline-study-saving-change-mali-results-segou-expansion-zone-and-existing-sfc-s>

CARE (2011) *2011 Microfinance in Africa: State-of-the-Sector Report: Closing the Gap*. Retrieved from: <www.care.org/getinvolved/advocacy/access-africa/pdf/CARE-Access-Africa-Closing-the-Gap-2011.pdf>

Catholic Relief Services (CRS) (2011) 'Financial education for children and youth', CRS. Retrieved from: <http://a4n.com.sv/uploaded/mod_documentos/CRS%20Children%20and%20youth%20savings.pdf>

Cohen, M. and Snodgrass, D. (2002) 'Clients in context: The impact of microfinance in three countries: A synthesis report', USAID AIMS.

Coulibaly, A. (2012) 'Access Africa. Impact of a VSLA Program: Evidence from CARE Rwanda SAFI project. Preliminary findings', CARE Kigali, unpublished.

DAI (2010) 'Group savings and loans associations: Impact study'. Retrieved from: <www.fsdkenya.org/pdf_documents/11-01-19_GSL_Impact_assessment_study.pdf>

Dills, L., Mayson, M., and Mukankusi, A. (2009) 'Increasing savings and solidarity among households with orphans and vulnerable children in Rwanda', Microfinance Learning Paper Series No. 3, CRS. Retrieved from: <www.crsprogramquality.org/storage/pubs/microfinance/Rwanda%20Learning%20Paper_web.pdf>

Deubel, T. and Nowak, B. (2012) 'Women's participation and exclusion in Saving for Change groups in pastoralist and migrant communities in Northwestern Mali', submitted to Oxfam America, unpublished.

Edwards, R. (2010) 'Saving for change in Mali: A study of atypical groups from Sikasso to Kayes'. Retrieved from: <http://savings-revolution.org/doclib/4-SfC-MALI-Atypical-Cases-FINAL.pdf>

Emerging Markets Consulting (EMC) and Wancer, M. (no date) 'Saving for Change's research study in Banteay Mean Chey and Kampot provinces. Final report – evaluation and baseline', Oxfam America.

Ferguson, M. (2012) 'Poverty outreach in fee-for-service savings groups'. Retrieved from: <www.crsprogramquality.org/publications/2012/2/21/poverty-outreach-in-fee-for-service-savings-groups.html>

Fleischer Proaño, L., Gash, M., and Kuklewiez, A. (2010) 'Strengths, weaknesses and evolution of the Peace Corps' 11-year old savings group program in Ecuador', Freedom from Hunger Research Report No. 13, FFH, Davis, CA.

Freedom from Hunger (FFH) (2011a) 'AIM Youth News: Advancing integrated microfinance for youth'. Retrieved from: <www.freedomfromhunger.org/pdfs/AIM_Youth_Newsletter_Aug2011_Eng.pdf>

FFH (2011b) 'Plan WARO: Youth microfinance project. Financial education needs assesment report', unpublished.

FFH and AIM Youth (no date) 'Saving for Change for youth: At-a-glance. A component of Advancing Integrated Microfinance for Youth (AIM Youth)'.

Hendricks, L. and Jain, A. (2005) SIMBA – supporting the income and basic needs of AIDS-affected households in Zimbabwe, *Small Enterprise Development* 16(3): 39–46.

Johnson, S. (2004) Gender norms in financial markets: evidence from Kenya, *World Development* 32(8): 1355–74.

Johnson, S. and Sharma, N. (2007) '"Institutionalizing suspicion": The management and governance challenge in user-owned microfinance groups', in T. Dichter and M. Harper (eds) *What's Wrong with Microfinance?*, pp. 61–72, Practical Action Publishing, Rugby.

Johnson, S., Brown, G., and Fouillet, C. (2012) 'The search for financial inclusion in Kenya's financial landscape: the rift revealed', FSD Kenya, Nairobi. Retrieved from: <www.fsdkenya.org/pdf_documents/12-03-29_Full_FinLandcapes_report.pdf>

Kaminaga, A., Devietti, E., Umul, C., and Matuszeski, J. (2011) 'Saving for Change in Guatemala baseline study', unpublished.

Malkamaki, M. (2010) 'The group savings and loans model in Kenya: Saving for change or failing to change?'.

Miller, J. and Gash, M. (2010) 'Saving for Change impact stories research: Extended report', Freedom from Hunger Research Paper No. 14., FFH, Davis, CA. Retrieved from: <www.ffhtechnical.org/resources/research-reports/isaving-changei-impact-stories>

Mukankusi A., Mayson, M., Caso, T., and Rowe, W.A. (2009) 'Empowering Rwandan youth through savings-led-microfinance', Catholic Relief Services, Baltimore, MD. Retrieved from: <www.crsprogramquality.org/storage/pubs/microfinance/MF%20Rwanda%20Case%20Study_for_web.pdf>

Nelson, C. and Butzberger, B. (2011). 'Savings, financial education, and social support for adolescent girls', Burundi process documentation, CARE Burundi, unpublished report.

Odell, M. and Rippey, P. (2010) 'The permanence and value of savings groups in CARE Kenya's COSAMO program, Nyanza Province, Kenya', Aga Khan Development Network. Retrieved from: <www.mastercardfdn.org/pdfs/Kenya_85x11_LR.pdf>

Odera, R. and Muruka, G. (2007) 'Savings and internal lending communities (SILC) in Kenya: program review', CRS and MicroSave. Retrieved from: <www.microsave.org/sites/default/files/research_papers/SILC%20Program%20Review%20Kenya%20December%202007.pdf>

Parrot, L. (2008) 'Kibara Mission Hospital HIV Project, Tanzania: Phase II: Savings and internal lending communities', The SEEP Network and CRS. Retrieved from: <www.crsprogramquality.org/storage/pubs/microfinance/kibaramission.pdf>

Plan International Canada (2009) 'Final and approved proposal youth economic empowerment: An integrated approach addressing youth poverty in Niger, Senegal and Sierra Leone', unpublished.

Seng, S., Sean, V., Keartha, C., Sokhom, L., and Phira, P. (2007) 'Saving for self-reliance initiative in Cambodia: Qualitative evaluation report'. Retrieved from: <www.seepnetwork.org/saving-for-self-reliance-initiative-in-cambodia-qualitative-evaluation-report-resources-738.php>

Umoh, M. and Bakliwal, S. (2011) 'A sustainable access to financial services for investment (SAFI) project: Learning document on poverty targeting and financial inclusion', CARE Rwanda. Retrieved from: <http://savings-revolution.org/doclib/>

Valley Research Group (VRG) and Mayoux, L. (2008) 'Women ending poverty: The WORTH Program in Nepal: Empowerment through literacy, banking and business 1999–2007'. Retrieved from: <www.pactworld.org/galleries/worth-files/Nepal_Final_Report_Letter_0825_PDF.pdf>

Van der Riet, M. (2009) 'SaveAct survey report', unpublished.

Vanmeenen, G. (2010) 'Savings and internal lending communities – SILC: Voices from Africa: The benefits of integrating SILC into development programming'. Retrieved from: <http://edu.care.org/Documents/Savings%20and%20Internal%20Lending%20Communities%20in%20Africa.pdf>

Winnebah, T. (2011) 'Youth Microfinance Project in Freetown, Sierra Leone: Baseline conditions of Youth Savings and Lending Associations' (YSLA) members', unpublished manuscript.

World Bank (2007) World Development Indicators. Retrieved from: <http://data.worldbank.org/data-catalog/world-development-indicators> [accessed 10 June 2012].

Zollmann, J. (2010) 'Waiting for the rain, reaching for mangoes: The origins, evolution, and roles of savings groups in rural Swaziland', Student Research Series, Center for Emerging Markets Enterprises, Tufts University, Medford, MA. Retrieved from: <http://fletcher.tufts.edu/CEME/publications/~/media/Fletcher/Microsites/CEME/pubs/pdfs/Student%20Pubs%20Zollman%20Mangoes.pdf>

About the authors

Susan Johnson is a senior lecturer in international development at the University of Bath. She has a background in economics and agricultural economics, and worked in development organizations for eight years before joining academia. She has researched and written extensively in the field of microfinance, expanding the analysis in this field to the institutional analysis of local financial markets – in particular, examining their social embeddedness. She has undertaken extensive research into microfinance and financial access, particularly on their gender dimensions, the role of informal financial services, and the impact of interventions on poverty. She has worked on a number of major impact assessment studies for DFID and the Ford Foundation, and has undertaken research on financial access and the development of decentralized financial systems with the Financial Sector Deepening Trust in Kenya.

Silvia Storchi received her Master's degree in well-being and human development from the University of Bath in 2010. Since then she has been working in South Africa as an intern with the Small Enterprise Foundation (SEF), and is currently carrying out research and monitoring and evaluation for SaveAct, an organization implementing savings groups in the provinces of Kwazulu-Natal and the Eastern Cape. She is also collaborating with ACAF Italia in the promotion of savings groups in Italy.

CHAPTER 3

Making it happen: approaches to group formation

Paul Rippey and Hugh Allen

Facilitating agencies use a diverse array of delivery channels to set up savings groups. This chapter looks at the cost and sustainability of these channels in the context of the expanding savings group movement.

Although savings groups are created by many different facilitating agencies (FAs), their structures are remarkably similar and are based on a common set of principles, the most fundamental of which are self-management and self-capitalization. Against this backdrop of commonality, a diverse array of delivery channels – the methods and processes used to mobilize and train savings groups – has evolved. FAs no longer question whether SGs are an efficient way to bring financial services to their members; they have moved on to the question of how best to form them. FAs are experimenting with inter-institutional arrangements, management and supervisory structures, incentives, training approaches, and messaging. Greater understanding of these elements may lead to a consensus on which of the diverse delivery channels is most successful in providing sustainable, affordable, high-quality financial services through SGs. Or, perhaps, some FAs will adopt multiple delivery channels, depending on their particular needs. It appears that several approaches can work quite well; the industry has gone forward with certain assumptions while continually looking for new information that can help practitioners to refine their choices.

This chapter presents both what is known about delivery channels on the basis of evidence, and what is believed on the basis of anecdote and principle. We trace the evolution of delivery channels and how their development has impacted cost and sustainability, two key considerations as facilitating agencies seek the subsidies required to expand and solidify the emerging savings group movement.

Defining delivery channels

Approaches to savings group formation and training can be classified into two broad categories: *project-driven*[1], in which group formation is directed by an external organization, and *community-driven*, in which SGs form by community initiative, without external intervention. These working classifications sometimes overlap, and do not exhaust the possible ways that groups are formed. Nonetheless, they are useful for our discussion here. While most attention among donors, international NGOs (INGOs), and local NGOs has been directed toward project-driven group formation, the community-driven channel is hugely important. It is also clear that many projects form groups through a hybrid arrangement; some projects have integrated community-driven group formation, and a large number of groups have emerged as a result of systems left in place by facilitating agencies.

Project-driven delivery channel

'Delivery channel' implies, of course, that some product or service is being delivered to groups. The principal service SG projects provide is training. During the period in which the group is forming, learning, and practising procedures, the project provides technical and social support which continues intermittently until the first annual share-out. After that, ongoing support may include assistance during crises and subsequent share-outs. In addition, projects often require periodic data collection. We lump all this assistance together under the category of 'training', which is provided largely or exclusively by a single person, referred to here as the 'trainer' – in most cases, the person directly responsible for supervision, accounting, monitoring and reporting. Questions about delivery channels often focus on the profile necessary for a successful trainer, and how that person should be selected, trained, motivated, supported, and supervised.

How these trainers are trained is a crucial element in ensuring quality training and supervision, which in turn supports groups in offering their members sustainable financial services. Many SG trainers have been trained by facilitating agencies practising a particular model, but more often they are at least one generation away from the facilitating agency. In other cases, members have been trained by someone who has simply read a manual and visited some groups, which, in the experience of the authors, produces groups with more variation in procedure. Projects have used trainers of different educational levels, ranging from high school dropouts to college graduates. Trainers with higher levels of education tend to more easily learn about and deliver additional (usually non-financial) services to groups.

The increasing use of village agents and community volunteers – trainers selected from the groups – has produced trainers who often have fewer academic credentials, but excellent motivation and empathy for the groups. Training these trainers involves more hands-on field experience than formal classroom work. In Kenya, Catholic Relief Services (CRS) significantly changed its recruitment process for trainers after realizing that it would be beneficial to ask the communities to identify good candidates, especially because those selected would graduate to working as Private Service Providers. In the PSP role, trainers would organize and support SGs on a fee-for-service basis. CRS ended up choosing agents who were less educated, but more tied to the community.[2]

Table 3.1 Evolution of delivery channels

Institutional arrangements	Trainer type
INGOs start out implementing directly	Facilitating agencies hire paid project staff to create and supervise SGs until they are independent
INGOs work with local partners to reduce costs, operate with greater agility, and save time in ramping up outreach	Project staff identify, train, and supervise community-based trainers (CBTs) who replace paid project staff as SG trainers
INGOs becoming facilitating agencies work in many countries as technical support agencies, mobilizing and investing donor funds across multiple projects	CBTs become independent service providers, some by design, some as a result of project closure. These community-based trainers may be volunteers or may generate fee income from the groups they train
National NGOs independently adopt an SG model and operate at much lower cost per member	National NGOs are beginning to work with CBTs, but also use their own staff, who may be salaried while grant funding is available and work as volunteers during the period between grants

Savings groups are successful to the extent that they receive the right messages and training from trainers, making trainer selection and preparation an important element in project success.

While the *work* of the trainer is essential to maintain quality SGs, the *cost* of the trainer is of secondary importance because it is usually a relatively small part of the total budget for savings group projects.[3] Much more important is the trainer's productivity, because the number of trainers needed to reach a certain number of groups has cascading effects on project costs for supervision, transportation, and back-office functions. Sometimes, the best strategy for reducing programme costs is to retain a smaller number of highly productive, better-paid trainers.

While there are countless institutions forming and training SGs today using a wide variety of approaches (discussed later), the arrangements presented in Table 3.1 and in the following discussion constitute not only a way of classifying project-driven delivery channels, but also to some extent present an evolutionary history of approaches. The delivery channels described first are generally the earlier approaches, now largely abandoned; the channels described later are more prominent today.

While a variety of institutional arrangements are still being practiced, there is a clear tendency toward working through local partners and CBTs, which is seen as a way to drive down costs and leave behind an institutional system that can potentially continue to create new SGs; CBTs are seen as a self-sustaining training and support capacity embedded at the community level.[4]

Direct implementation

In CARE Niger's Mata Masu Dubara (MMD), the SG project that was the precursor to modern savings groups, there was a direct and simple approach to motivating and monitoring the trainer: a foreign donor gave money to

CARE Niger, and CARE Niger paid staff to train groups. The use of staff trainers facilitated a common approach, and it was much too early in the development of the SG discipline for CARE to be concerned about measuring or comparing cost per member. It is not surprising that the innovators in the field used their own staff; no one realized that this new SG model would become a replicable approach, standardized through manuals and spread through training.

However, it became clear that direct implementation by salaried INGO trainers had significant disadvantages in terms of cost and performance: INGO personnel costs are usually high, and on average, CBTs paid by groups equal or out-perform paid project staff in terms of the amount of savings mobilized, average loan size, and return on assets (www.thesavix.org).

With time, the architecture of delivery channels has become more complicated. Transnational structures, here called 'meta-projects', have been inserted into the chain between the donor and the country programme.

Transnational structures

Several of the most prominent INGOs, notably AKF, CARE, CRS, Plan, and, more recently, World Vision, have created transnational structures with some or all of the following objectives:

- defining an institution-wide strategy related to SG programming;
- developing a brand to motivate staff, unify approaches, and use in marketing;
- helping country programmes develop their national SG strategies;
- providing consistent, programme-wide technical support in partner selection, project design, methodological training, monitoring, and evaluation, including MIS training and impact studies;
- mobilizing resources; and
- collecting and aggregating data.

While the most prominent of these meta-projects is CARE's Access Africa programme covering 36 countries, CRS and Plan International have also achieved broad presence across Africa and elsewhere with programmes in 34 and 25 countries respectively. In addition, the Saving for Change consortium[5] has a very large-scale programme in seven countries, and World Vision has planned to invest in a major scaling-up of its SG work worldwide.

These international agencies work with the most vulnerable populations, offering a model by which they can access financial services; some have included other development services in health, literacy, or agricultural promotion and marketing. Savings groups work well as platforms for additional services because their normally difficult-to-reach members meet regularly in fixed locations, they are organized and disciplined, and they already have bonds of trust with their NGO partners – all of which facilitates service delivery.

In some cases, the integration of multiple services starts with a project in another sector that adds SGs to its design. Whether operating SGs through standalone projects or integrating them into other livelihood or social development activities, the decision by so many players to invest in transnational SG support structures attests to the importance of this approach in their overall programming.

While these transnational structures have been essential to the growth of the SG movement, it is possible that they will have accomplished their missions in the medium-term, as donors, country programmes, and local partners all become more familiar and comfortable with the SG concept and are independently able to relate to each other and generate financial support. It is also likely that the facilitating agencies' focus will shift from a narrow attention to methodology and a limited set of financial services, to a greater interest in the development of collateral services that can be delivered through SGs – with all of the implied risks and opportunities. Adding on services may result in the SG project changing focus, changing its strategy to attain sustainability, or introducing new and unfamiliar technologies and services. As the responsibility for project implementation shifts more and more toward partners, INGOs become increasingly interested in research and experimentation. It is possible that donor interest will also begin to move more decisively towards direct engagement with projects and partners that have been 'incubated' by the facilitating agencies.

Subcontracts with local NGOs and other partners

International NGOs often work through local partners, but it was only after the approaches to savings group formation and training became standardized and simplified that INGOs began to rely systematically on local partners to form and train groups.[6] CARE Uganda was among the first to adopt this approach, having launched a large project built on a local partner model in 2005. At much the same time, and independently, Plan International developed programmes working exclusively through partners in all of its 43 west African projects. Since 2006, CRS has worked through 187 Diocesan partners in all of its SG programming in 27 countries. Thus, a consensus is emerging among the larger INGOs that working through local partners is a practical approach to cutting costs,[7] setting up operations more rapidly, and working with greater geographic agility. In addition, some INGOs have a stated mission to build the capacity of local organizations, and the partnership model helps them to achieve that objective.

In this model, the local partners receive training from the INGO and use their own staff to form the groups. They typically use their own copy of an industry-standard MIS jointly financed and developed by VSL Associates, CARE, Oxfam, CRS, Plan International, and the Bill & Melinda Gates Foundation, and send their reports to the facilitating agency. Consolidated project reports are sent upstream, eventually arriving at the SAVIX website,[8] a portal for financial and statistical data on SGs around the world.

The partner approach has lowered costs of SG projects, as local NGOs' expenses for salaries and transportation tend to be lower than those of INGOs.

Significantly, this approach has led to the continuation of services after project funding ends, because most of the local partners are better-positioned to continue forming and supporting groups.

Subcontracting also has its costs, of course. Working with multiple local partners and managing numerous sub-grants is labour-intensive; the INGO must invest in training for the partner organization staff to ensure group quality, collection of accurate financial data, and correct use of the MIS.

Community-based trainers

The original concept of using community-based trainers (CBTs) was developed by CARE Niger and has been widely adopted, in different forms, across the sector. Recognizing that paid project staff could not meet the rapidly growing demand for SG training, CARE Niger selected CBTs from groups that had been trained by a paid field officer. After a period of supervision, trainers were free to create their own groups on a fee-for-service basis.[9] Community-based trainers now exist under different names; some are paid, some are volunteers. They offer the advantage of a low-cost local presence that can contribute to cultivating and sustaining an SG culture. Variations in the CBT model are discussed in the following sections.

Saving for Change community volunteers

The Saving for Change (SfC) Consortium, which promotes SGs in Mali, uses unpaid community volunteers to form additional groups. Chosen by the programme from among group members, these volunteers are called 'replicating agents'. SfC's approach is to train one group in the village, and then invite replicating agents from the formally trained group to set up other groups in the village. The paid SfC trainer supports the replicating agent as needed. Technically, the replicating agents can operate on their own once they have been trained to use a simplified pictorial manual to form groups. The process is 'front-loaded' with training, followed by a light touch with no defined limits on how long the SfC trainer can continue to contact the replicating agents. While the replicating agents often receive small gifts from the groups they train, the motivation for their work is clearly more intrinsic than financial, expressed in terms of improved social standing and the satisfaction of helping their relatives and neighbours.

Fee-for-service trainers

Both INGOs and local partners are increasingly using fee-for-service (FFS) models, in which the trainers are paid not by the project (although in some cases they receive a stipend for the first year or two), but rather are paid by the groups themselves. Of course, the line between volunteers and fee-for-service trainers is not always clear. FFS trainers report that they are also motivated by the same intrinsic factors of satisfaction and helping others as the volunteers are, and volunteers report that they feel incentivized when they receive material support from groups in the form of tea or cola, money for transport, or a gift at the share-out.

The FFS approach has been widely adopted in different forms by CARE, Plan, and CRS. It usually requires identification, training, and supervision of FFS trainers for a limited period by salaried INGO or local NGO trainers. Many INGOs now consider this approach a practical exit strategy that leaves in place a self-financing means to continue group replication and maintain periodic support to groups (such as at the annual share-out, at the annual review of a group's constitution, or in helping with occasional conflict resolution). CRS's SILC programme in Kenya, Tanzania, and Uganda was designed to test the viability of a fee-for-service model; it includes a thoughtful step-by-step process for training, certifying, and launching 'Private Service Providers' who organize and support SGs on a commercial basis.[10]

The use of fee-for-service trainers is sometimes influenced by the intentions of the local partner to remain in contact with post-project groups. While INGOs will frequently train groups and then have little contact with them past the end of the funded project, local NGOs are more likely to follow a 'train and retain' model, in which they stay in contact with groups indefinitely and use them as a conduit for various sorts of development aid. The local NGOs often see the network of rural savings groups they have developed as an asset; they can use their ability to reach a large number of organized, disciplined group members as a selling point when they are marketing their services to donors. These considerations mediate in favour of keeping field staff in contact with their groups post-project. Fee-for-service models are sometimes the least expensive, or even the only affordable way to maintain these relationships. As a result, some local NGO staff transition to fee-for-service trainers after the end of the project funding.

Evidence from limited studies indicates that this approach can be effective in multiplying programme results post-project, at little or no cost to donors (Anyango et al., 2007). Remaining questions relate to the longevity and performance of groups created in this way, and to the possible dampening effects of fee-for-service trainers on the creation of spontaneous groups.

Table 3.2 Comparison of group performance: paid project staff vs. CBTs

Metric	Field officer: project paid	Village agent: group paid
Total no. of groups	14,354	8,424
Savings as percentage of loans outstanding (%)	155.5	166.3
Savings per member, as percentage of GNI per capita (%)	7.0	8.5
Average outstanding loan size, as percentage of GNI per capita (%)	6.3	8.0
Members with loans outstanding (%)	46.4	41.0
Loans outstanding as percentage of performing assets (%)	51.6	49.8
Annualized return on assets	37.5	44.4

Source: www.thesavix.org

What is becoming clear, however, is that CBTs paid by the groups they train may be out-performing paid project staff in terms of key performance indicators. Taken on average, groups trained by CBTs appear to mobilize more savings, have members who tend to borrow in larger amounts, and are more profitable (see Table 3.2).

Outsourced CBTs (CARE's COSALO model)

CARE's COSALO project in Kenya pioneered a model through which many of the functions of group formation were outsourced to local entrepreneurs and faith-based organizations (FBOs) that contracted and supervised SG trainers. CARE paid a commission per member trained, which was divided between the trainer and the entrepreneur or FBO. The project reported remarkable output, with the cost per member well under $10. In some cases, the entrepreneurs and their trainers found innovative ways to train groups as quickly as possible to gain the greatest commissions. Some of the positive innovations include the massive clustering of groups to both reduce the number of visits and encourage inter-group learning, the use of radio spots, and systematic visits to weekly markets to recruit new groups. Other innovations – including emphasis on monthly rather than weekly meetings, the optional use of lockboxes, and the adoption of a uniform savings amount for all members in place of the variable and flexible share system – cut corners in ways that were probably not in the members' best interests. Yet, despite some flaws, the remarkable efficiency of outsourcing makes it a possible model for other projects.

Community-driven delivery channel

When savings groups are introduced into an area, very often, members go on to form other groups. This often happens without the awareness of the FA or project. Two studies in western Kenya have shown the scope of this phenomenon. In one district, Odell and Rippey (2011) found 37 groups that had been created by members of the 44 groups formed by CARE.[11] In a 2011 study, also in western Kenya, Financial Sector Deepening (FSD) Kenya and Digital Divide Data specifically looked for evidence of replication in a sample of 54 groups. They found that 'Replication was the norm, with the average group creating nearly two additional groups in the 14 months since the project ended. Three-quarters of all groups had replicated' (FSD/Digital Divide Data, 2011). It is not known to what extent western Kenya is representative of other parts of the world, of course, but most projects have shown some evidence of community-driven group formation.

Even before SfC started employing the volunteer model described in the section above, it reported an annually compounded rate of group-to group formation that exceeded 30 per cent in Mali.[12] Realizing the promise of this model, SfC shifted to a community-based trainer model to reach expansion targets under its Gates Foundation grant, which called for programme growth at a rate of 10,000 new members per month.

Since community-driven group formation is such a strong motor of expansion, especially in Africa,[13] an important question is whether to encourage or discourage it, and how to ensure the quality of groups formed by other groups.

Odell and Rippey (2011) identified four ways in which savings groups form new savings groups:

1. *Fission of large groups*. As groups add members, they get unwieldy and sometimes split into two or more groups, which often keep the same name, calling themselves groups A, B, C, and so on. These groups will often share some functions, like a common social fund, and sometimes an overall governing body.
2. *Splinter groups*. Sometimes members leave a group because of dissatisfaction with some element of the original group – such as its management, disruptive members, or location – and start their own group, which often grows in membership over time.
3. *Social entrepreneurs*. In some cases, dynamic local people have taken it upon themselves to form additional groups as a civic service. This is the case with the Saving for Change replicating agents.
4. *ROSCA upgrading*. Sometimes a member of a savings group who belongs to a ROSCA introduces the SG approach to the ROSCA members, who decide to adopt it.

The FSD/Digital Divide Data study (2011) identified additional variants:

1. *Natal village*. Women who move to their husband's village go back to visit their families, and while they are there share what they have learned about savings groups.
2. *'Inspired by'*. Some groups are formed with no real input from existing groups, but simply because neighbours have carefully observed meetings and imitated the procedures.
3. *Other upgraded*. Just as ROSCAs sometimes choose to upgrade to an SG, other sorts of groups – women's, youth, CBOs – may also adopt the SG methodology.
4. *Clusters*. Very often, groups meet at the same time and in the same place, sometimes in a church hall or civic centre, sometimes outside, forming a cluster of groups. Clusters' visibility and dynamism act as a magnet to new members, and clusters have grown, in some cases, to 12 or more member groups.

Relationship among project-driven and community-driven channels

It is likely that the facilitating agency's system and messages about replication influence the rate and quality of community-driven group formation. Table 3.3 shows some ways an FA *might* encourage or discourage the community to form SGs, through its choice of message and approach.

Table 3.3 Messages and approaches that can influence community-driven SG formation

Message	Encouraging approach	Discouraging approach
The difficulty of running an SG	This is easy and we will show you how to do it	This is difficult, but we will show you how to do it
Replication	This is so easy you can show your neighbour how to do it	If your neighbour sees you and wants to start a group, let me know and I'll help them
The relationship between the FA and the SG	Once you learn how to do this, you will be independent	Once you learn the basics, we'll be back to show you more
Standard of boxes and passbooks	Simple, local, and inexpensive	Fancy or complex, imported from the capital city, and expensive
Access to boxes, passbooks	Available through the private sector	Available only through project
Bookkeeping system	Passbooks and oral	Ledgers, or ledgers plus passbooks

No reliable research has been done to inform how community-driven group formation is affected by project-driven group formation, rendering the preceding table hypothetical; readers should form their own conclusions pending more research. Some studies in Mali and Kenya due in 2012 and 2013 will begin to shine some light on this question.[14]

Even if appropriate messages and approaches can significantly encourage community-driven group creation, there is still legitimate debate about whether and how savings groups should be encouraged to form new groups, or whether that task should be left to trained trainers. The strong argument for encouraging community-driven group formation is that it turns the SG into a community asset, one that is more likely to remain part of the culture and continue to be available to new people. The argument against encouraging community-driven group formation is that community groups are likely to differ from project-driven groups in various ways – adapting the rules to fit their preferences, or forgoing certain parts of the training.[15] The study in Kenya found that community-driven groups were hungry for formal training, especially in recordkeeping, and would likely be willing to pay in order to have at least a few members trained (FSD/Digital Divide Data, 2011).

Mobile phones: increasing the efficiency of service delivery

Although they are not a delivery channel, mobile phones merit attention because the rapidly evolving technology will insert itself into SG operations, and potentially influence service delivery. In fact, in March 2012, CARE Kenya, Orange (a mobile telephone company), and Equity Bank launched a new product designed especially for savings groups, with features that mimic their emblematic lockboxes (see Chapter 1, Ledgerwood and Jethani (2013), for a full description).

In addition, efforts are underway to develop software through which phones could carry out SG recordkeeping functions. Any telephone application used for recordkeeping is likely also to have a remote reporting function, and could be set up to report balances, attendance, and other group quality measures automatically.

If savings groups follow the same path taken by others, it is likely that electronic media will replace other media – that is, electronic transfers will steadily overtake cash transactions, and digital recordkeeping will replace pen, stamp, and paper. However, as useful as the new electronic media are, they do not constitute a 'channel', but rather convenient tools that can increase efficiency, savings mobilization, security, and transparency.

And, it should be stressed mobile banking cannot by itself replace savings groups, because it does not provide one of their key features: the use of peer pressure to instill savings discipline. In fact, first-generation mobile accounts have been likened to expensive digital wallets; they are too liquid to satisfy the preference for illiquidity, which is driven by the need to lock up savings so they will accumulate into the larger lump sums necessary for emergencies and investments.[16] But technology will continue to march on, and powerful synergies are likely to arise when the security and cost advantages of mobile-phone savings transactions are combined with the peer-pressure savings expectations of a savings group.

Cost of training members

The choice of delivery channel is motivated in large part by efforts to decrease the cost of training group members, an objective shared by both facilitating agencies and donors. At present, all facilitating agencies posting their data to the SAVIX have agreed to use a standardized approach to calculate cost per member (CPM). Facilitating agencies calculate their total project costs – including all those incurred by their partner organizations – and allocate them, proportionate to the number of members, across an array of projects. They exclude all research and evaluation costs that do not relate directly to project implementation, as well as the proportion of costs that can be assigned to an SG programme in cases where activities that span multiple sectors result in shared administrative and capital costs. However, at the level of individual projects, decisions on how to assign costs are left to the projects themselves, and tools are available to assist in the process.

While the process certainly includes anomalies and different interpretations of shared costs, its wide acceptance has led to an approximate similarity of approach to calculating costs. However, a multitude of exceptions make the cost-per-member calculation subject to inconsistent application. For example, paid field staff may work on multiple project activities, some of which do not relate to creating SGs. Or they may work on activities such as small business or literacy training, or commission-based sales of solar lamps or other socially desirable products that both take up their time and bring in revenue that offsets their costs. Computing cost per member with precision is not an easy task, and, therefore, its use must be nuanced. Table 3.4 shows nine factors affecting CPM that must be taken into account.

Table 3.4 Nine factors affecting calculation of cost per member (CPM)

Factor	Discussion
Programme maturity and project infrastructure	The time between the beginning of a project and the formation of the first groups can have a significant impact on CPM; start-up programmes are inevitably more expensive because the facilitating agency has to put in place the basic project infrastructure, from hiring staff to renting offices. If a new project follows an earlier project in the same area, it can take advantage of the existing staff and other infrastructure.
Scale	Some economies of scale, such as management, IT, accounting, and administration expenses can be spread over a larger number of members.
Geography	Dense and accessible populations are generally less expensive to reach than sparse populations in difficult-to-reach areas.
Exchange rate	Comparing CPM in dollars is unfavourable to countries with expensive currencies.
Other services	Many projects either add a savings group component to projects providing other services, in sectors like agriculture, health, and education, or add other services to SG projects, using the groups as a platform to gain rapid outreach. The manner of accounting for the two services is in practice a matter of choice for the FA, which can bring the CPM down by attributing more of the costs to the other activity, or can justify the other activity by accounting for it as an opportunistic and serendipitous add-on with low marginal cost. Some add-ons, including the increasingly popular solar lamp sales through SGs,[17] can bring in revenue that actually offsets some project costs, and thus reduces CPM.
Self-reporting	While there are guidelines for computing costs, reporting is left to the FA, and allows a certain amount of liberty in how to account for other services, monitoring and evaluation, home office oversight, multiple-country programmes, and long-term investments.
Multiple membership	Like the question of cost calculation, the calculation of number of members is hardly free of nuance. Some projects tolerate members being in multiple groups, and many members cheerfully belong to two, three, or more groups. The standard MIS reports the number of memberships, but cannot detect if the same person belongs to two or more SGs. Some programmes have gone to the tedious and expensive length of maintaining a separate database listing all members, but even this measure cannot easily detect multiple memberships when many people have the same name, not everyone has a national ID number, or the spelling of the same name can vary.
Post-project group formation, spontaneous group formation	Fee-for-service (FFS) projects, and particularly CRS, reasonably argue that the membership variable should include post-project group formation, because their model makes heavy investments in the development of trainers who are trained and mentored to create sustainable businesses training new groups indefinitely.[18] How to account for these groups raises all sorts of questions: over what period should one expect the trainers to be productive? Should future groups have a discounted value compared to present groups? How does one determine the net contribution of FFS trainers, since in many areas there is a large amount of spontaneous group formation, in the absence of any trainers? How should quality be weighted, given the substantial evidence that groups formed by trainers respect procedures much more than groups formed by the community? How should one value the other services that FFS trainers provide, including help with share-out?
Record accuracy	Data with little relationship to reality are sometimes reported either inadvertently or deliberately.

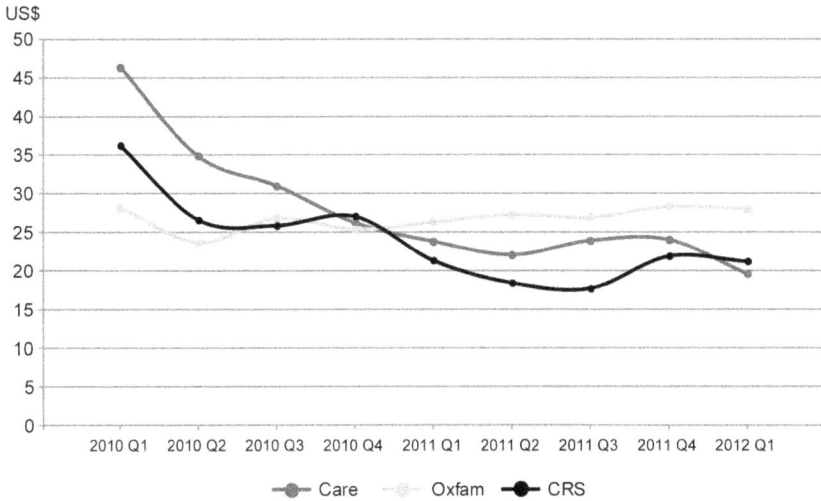

Figure 3.1 Cost per member assisted, by agency

While issues remain around calculation, cost per member has settled at an average of about $20–25 a head, during the lifetime of a three to four-year project implemented by an international facilitating agency, usually through partners (see Figure 3.1). But some projects are substantially below that mark (donors are exerting pressure on FAs to reduce their CPM to the $15 range, or less). While such expectations may or may not be reasonable (and there is passionate debate about this), it seems likely that costs will tend toward a lower level, especially when SG projects are directly implemented by a southern NGO. For example, Dutabarane in Burundi has been able to deliver good results at about half the lowest cost of most INGO-funded programmes. How, then, will donors relate to the southern programmes that are beginning to produce high-quality groups at much lower cost than INGO facilitating agencies?

Defining sustainability

When applied to traditional microfinance institutions, *sustainability* has a fairly clear meaning: an MFI is considered to be sustainable if it earns enough money to cover its costs, and no other internal weaknesses or external threats are likely to put it out of business in the medium term.

This concept is not easily transferrable to savings groups because multiple definitions are relevant. We address four of them: financial sustainability and sustainability as defined by survivability over time, a concept with three levels.

In a financial sense, most SGs certainly are sustainable: their few operating costs are easily covered by their revenues. In fact, SGs typically have a very high return on investment for their members. The SAVIX database indicates that all reporting projects have an average return of 36.8 per cent.[19] Those few SGs that suffer losses through theft or portfolio weakness might show a loss for the cycle. Fortunately, these catastrophic losses are rare, and anecdotal evidence suggests that many groups manage to survive them, as the members bravely regroup and keep saving. Other groups wind up operations if they lose their money.[20]

Despite impressive financial returns, a common question is 'how long do SGs survive?' Odell and Rippey (2010) contend that sustainability is not only a question of long-term survival, since group membership is often in a state of flux. They distinguish three levels of sustainability: that of the group, that of access, and that of the concept.

Group sustainability. This refers to the continued existence of the group after the end of training. There is substantial evidence that in most projects, most groups exist indefinitely. Further research currently underway in multiple countries including Mali and Kenya[21] should soon begin to quantify the survival rate of groups. The SAVIX panel study of 332 groups so far shows that only six groups ceased to operate after two years. Two of these are reported to have merged with other groups. In the first long-term study of savings groups after the facilitating agency (CARE) had ceased to work in the area ('Village Savings and Loan Associations: Experience from Zanzibar'), the authors found that all 43 original groups had survived (although one had closed and re-formed). The total number of members had increased by 256 per cent; in 2009 there were reported to be more than 250 groups. None were reported to have shut down (Anyango et al., 2007).[22]

Permanence of member access. If members continue to have access to services from a savings group, it is less important whether individual groups continue to exist. The change in total membership post-project is an indicator of sustainability of access. The COSALO study shows steady growth in member access despite the fact that group membership and identity were very fluid, as groups splintered, members moved around, and names were changed (Digital Divide Data, 2011). Nevertheless, even if member access continues to grow, the fate of individual groups is still important because the circumstances in which a group ceases to exist might easily be injurious to the interests of the members.

Permanence of the concept. Questions remain about the permanence of the concept, or the degree to which groups stay true to principles and practices in which they were trained. Two studies from Kenya have tried to measure the extent to which groups deviate from standard procedures. DAI found 'questions about a basic CARE premise: the ability of incubated savings groups to resist "entropy" or loss of compliance to the methodology derived from external training'. The DAI study found clear evidence of enormous diversity within the VSLA universe in the study area. Members ranked 'respect for the rules' ninth in order of governance priorities for their groups – a placement that may help to explain the process of 'entropy'. The study by FSD Kenya and Digital Divide Data found that second generation groups were less likely to meet punctually, use lock boxes, or respect formal procedures. What is not known is the extent to which this procedure drift affects the permanence of groups, the security of members' assets, or the return on investment. Many practices have been widely adopted, including lockboxes with three locks, use of passbooks, specific seating arrangements at meetings, and the order of the agenda items. These practices all make sense, and it is prudent for SGs to adopt them, but their effect on specific outcomes – while presumed – has not been measured. A common adage in advertising is that half of advertising budgets is wasted, but no one knows which half. Similarly, it is possible that half of the procedures followed are not necessary to favourable outcomes, but no one knows which half.

Conclusion: speculating about the next 20 years

What will the future look like? Perhaps the distinction between project-led and community-led delivery channels will become less distinct; as facilitating agencies leave SGs to function independently, their communities will take over the process and adopt, at least in part, the systems established to mobilize and support them. Much of the modern approach to savings groups was developed by groups themselves, and it would be a mistake to underestimate the ability of the collective intelligence of millions of members to come up with further innovations.

The externally supported trainer will likely be replaced by the community-based trainer, who will add payments from savings groups to her or his multiple sources of income. The outreach offered by savings groups makes them attractive platforms for marketing of ideas and products, and the CBT is the key connection to those platforms. If the INGO meta-projects are no longer needed to help form groups, they will either disappear from working themselves out of their jobs, or find new *raisons d'être*, perhaps in identifying new services and products to give or sell to savings groups.

In a future scenario in which the savings group has become embedded in the culture, the hot issue of cost per member may no longer be relevant. Sustainability of access will be achieved.

Finally, many groups will conduct their business using telephones – not today's phones, but rather the affordable smartphones of tomorrow, with purpose-built applications and capabilities and functions that we can only dream of.

Questions for further consideration

1. Since community-driven group formation is such a strong motor of expansion, should it be encouraged? If so, how can the quality of 'replicated' groups be ensured?
2. How is community-driven group formation affected by project-driven group formation?
3. The evolution toward fee-for-service training raises all sorts of questions:
   i.   Over what period should one expect the trainers to be productive?
   ii. In computing CPM, should future groups have a discounted value compared to present groups?

iii. How does one determine the *net* contribution of FFS trainers, since many areas witness a large amount of spontaneous group formation anyway, in the absence of any trainers?

iv. How should quality be weighted, given that there is substantial evidence that groups formed by trainers respect procedures better than groups formed by the community?

v. How should one value the other services that FFS trainers provide, including help with share-out?

4. What is the effect of the many prudent practices that have been widely adopted, including use of lockboxes with three locks, use of passbooks, specific seating arrangements at meetings, and the order of agenda items? Their effect on specific outcomes, while presumed, has not been measured. If savings groups, operating independently, adapt these procedures to their own liking for various reasons, will their outcomes be affected?

Acknowledgements

Early drafts of this chapter elicited many thoughtful and useful comments, and much vigorous discussion, both online and in email exchanges. The authors thank Jeffrey Ashe, marc bavois, Eloisa Devietti, Joanna Ledgerwood, Brian Lund, Candace Nelson, David Panetta, Laura Fleischer Proaño, Andrea Teebagy, and Guy Vanmeenen for their contributions.

Notes

1. We use the term 'project' in reference to implementation by a specific organization, such as Community Vision in Tororo, Uganda. An SG 'programme' is usually a set of SG projects, such as CARE Uganda's work through 29 different partners (one of whom is Community Vision).

2. J. Wangare Munene, Program Manager of SILC Innovations, Catholic Dioceses of Malindi, in conversation with Candace Nelson (February 2012).

3. Based on a number of project proposals, the range of total salary costs for paid project field staff appears to vary between 20–35 per cent of total project costs, depending on scale, duration, and the extent to which CBTs are used. Salary costs can be higher with small-scale, short-term pilot projects.

4. Some argue that, over time, the totality of groups trained by direct implementation and CBTs will represent a more cost-effective outcome, as post-project group creation will continue to drive down overall per-unit costs.

5. Oxfam America, Freedom from Hunger, and Stromme Foundation programme.

6. While programmes that have performed exceptionally well are usually involved in partnerships with local NGOs, there are other powerful factors that influence cost, not the least of which are programme age and scale.

7. There has been a general downward trend in cost per member assisted, as reported on savix.org, to an average of $25.20 across all of the 130 programmes contributing data. After pursuing a highly disciplined approach, CARE Uganda has brought its cost per person reported on the

SAVIX to $19.90 while CRS has steadily cut costs to an average of $17.70 across all three countries reporting (Kenya, Uganda, and Tanzania).

8. See Panetta, 2013, for an explanation of the SAVIX and other performance measurement tools used by SG facilitating agencies.

9. Most CBTs are paid as a flat fee per member, per meeting, usually taken from the SG's social fund or loan fund. The amount varies, but $0.025 per member is common.

10. CARE labels its FFS trainers as community-based trainers or village agents.

11. Furthermore, the authors were certain that they had not identified all of the community-driven groups, as exhaustive identification was not part of their study's purpose.

12. V. Parrneshwar, Deputy Director of Community Finance, Oxfam America, in conversation with Hugh Allen in 2010.

13. There is emerging evidence that the replication model is also working, although to a lesser extent, in Central America.

14. A planned household study in Kenya; the panel study of VSL Associates which is reporting on SG performance of 332 groups in six countries for five years; and an RCT being carried out in Mali by Innovations for Poverty Action based at Yale University to be completed in 2012.

15. Some would argue in favour of users modifying their group to make it match their preferences.

16. Morduch, J. and Rutherford, S. (November 2010), 'Financial Services for the Poor: Needs and Impact,' presentation at the Global Savings Forum, Gates Foundation, Seattle, WA. Their studies in Malawi indicate that an ordinary savings account increases investment in agriculture by 16 per cent, while adding a commitment savings account increases the level of investment by 48 per cent. They further show that while there is a negligible increase in crop sales with only an ordinary savings account, sales increased by 27 per cent when a commitment savings account was added. Food consumption rose, respectively, by 16 per cent and 25 per cent when ordinary and commitment products were combined.

17. See www.CleanAirBrightLight.org.

18. For example, it cost CARE over $240 per member in its Zanzibar project in 2000–02, a sum that neither CARE nor any other agency would spend now; at the end of the project, CARE left behind a fee-for-service structure, and the original 43 groups have grown to more than 250 while the amount of capital mobilized and managed by the average group has tripled, all at no further cost to CARE. Even the high costs per member of a decade ago seem reasonable when post-project growth is taken into account.

19. Annualized return on total assets. Returns on savings will be higher, as will return on average assets, which are not as yet calculated by the SAVIX.

20. Susan Johnson has pointed out that failed groups of all kinds are under-reported, since evaluators find it easier to visit groups that are still in operation, than those that have failed (Johnson et. al., 2010).

21. The Bill & Melinda Gates Foundation has supported VSL Associates in conducting quantitative research on SGs in multiple countries. DfID's Financial Sector Deepening programme in Kenya is also sponsoring several studies of SGs.

22. Note that the Zanzibar study covered a small single project and, while the SAVIX panel study covers a large number of groups in several countries, its final results were not available to inform this discussion.

References

Anyango, E., Esipisu, E., Opoku, L., Johnson, S., Malkamaki, M., and Musoke, C. (2007) 'Village savings and loan associations: Experience from Zanzibar' *Small Enterprise Development* 18(1):11–24.

Digital Divide Data (2011) 'Results of study of post-project replication of groups in COSALO I', Financial Sector Deepening Kenya, Nairobi. Retrieved from: <www.fsdkenya.org/pdf_documents/12-01-20_COSALO_I_short_study.pdf>

Johnson, S., Malkamäki, M. and Niño-Zarazua, M. (2010) 'The role of informal groups in financial markets: Evidence from Kenya', Bath Papers in International Development, Centre for Development Studies, University of Bath. Retrieved from: <www.bath.ac.uk/cds/bpd/bpd7.pdf>

Ledgerwood, J. and Jethani, A. (2013) 'Savings groups and financial inclusion', in C. Nelson (ed.), *Savings Groups at the Frontier*, pp. 13–35, Practical Action Publishing, Rugby, UK.

Odell, M.K. and Rippey, P. (2011) 'The permanence and value of savings groups in CARE Kenya's COSAMO programme, Nyanza Province, Kenya' AKF Savings Group Learning Initiative, AKF Canada. Retrieved from: <www.mastercardfdn.org/pdfs/Kenya_85x11_LR.pdf>

Panetta, D. (2013) 'Performance monitoring', in C. Nelson (ed.), *Savings Groups at the Frontier*, pp. 127–146, Practical Action Publishing, Rugby, UK.

About the authors

Paul Rippey is a consultant specialized in savings groups, and particularly how they can be combined with other developmental activities. He has led training, evaluations, design and research missions in a dozen countries in Africa and Asia. He was a leader in introducing the notion of cost-per-member as an important, if imprecise, measure of efficiency. Paul is a founder of the Savings Revolution website, an independent forum for anyone interested in community-managed, savings-led approaches, and of www.CleanAirBrightLight.org, a site promoting the use of savings groups as a platform for the commercialization of clean lighting. He previously had a successful career working with top-down, credit-led institutions.

Hugh Allen has worked for 42 years on microfinance and technology-driven development. For 13 years he was CARE International's Technical Advisor on microenterprise development in Africa, where, in 1992, he first came across CARE Niger's MMD programme, subsequently helping to set up VSL projects in 16 other countries. In 2004 he founded VSL Associates, which specializes in the refinement and promotion of this methodology, and has worked in 38 countries. With donor assistance, Hugh has developed the industry MIS for Savings Groups, and the SAVIX website, measuring the performance of SG programmes worldwide. He is the author of *Village Savings & Loan Associations – A Practical Guide* (2007) and books on mass-market technologies. He is a contributing author to *What's Wrong with Microfinance?* (2007) and *Financial Promise for the Poor* (2010).

CHAPTER 4
Thrift-led development

Kim Wilson

The benefits of savings groups go beyond the financial to the social, with the cohesion and confidence of the group affecting the social and personal development of its members. This chapter looks at the many facets of social development that savings groups have promoted.

The chicken lays an egg and the egg hatches a chicken. So it is with groups. Savings begets confidence; confidence drives savings. Pinpointing which happy behaviour sparks which, in a virtuous cycle of thrift and empowerment, challenges the wisest expert. None have untangled the sheer power of thrift and borrowing from the sheer power of confidence and cohesion.

Though financial and social benefits might appear in a yin-yang relationship, as far as savings groups are concerned, they can and do exist separately. Many groups, particularly those in South Asia, might meet for months or even years, building group cohesion long before saving or borrowing a cent. In contrast, savings groups in Africa or Haiti, particularly those urged on by NGOs, begin saving and lending immediately.

Let us assume for this chapter that most groups save and lend soon into their journey, and that development emerges organically from member confidence and group unity as well as from access to savings, loans, and investment. When we talk about development, then, we are discussing not just economic growth, but also personal growth – for example, the pride that accompanies achievement, the ability to seize new opportunities, and the chance to join with others around a common cause. This chapter reviews what groups themselves, and NGOs that support them, do to promote development and tells a story about their conscious development efforts, beyond saving and lending.

Preamble – a typology of groups

Figure 4.1 illustrates some important extremes in the types of activities that groups undertake, as well as the level of outside support they garner. The horizontal logic differentiates groups by type of development activities undertaken, with the top row indicating strictly financial services and the bottom describing the incorporation of additional, non-financial development services for members, groups, and communities. The columns separate groups

Groups only do simple thrift, lending and distributions

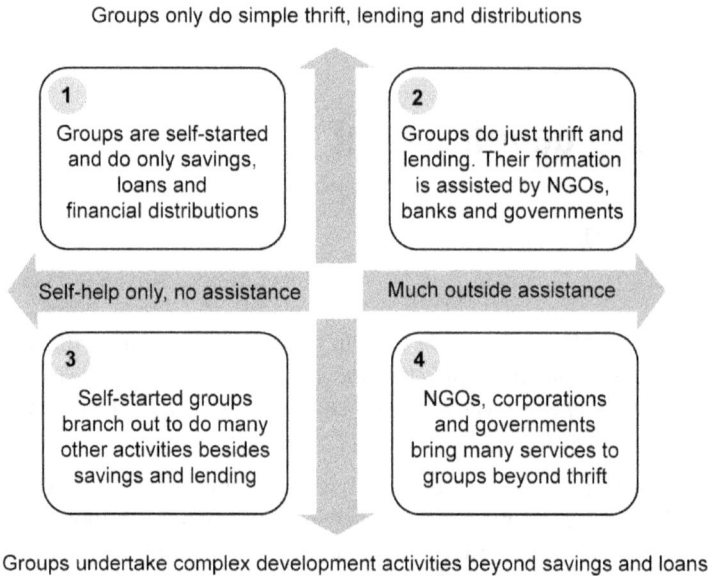

1

Groups are self-started
and do only savings,
loans and
financial distributions

2

Groups do just thrift and
lending. Their formation
is assisted by NGOs,
banks and governments

Self-help only, no assistance   Much outside assistance

3

Self-started groups
branch out to do many
other activities besides
savings and lending

4

NGOs, corporations
and governments
bring many services to
groups beyond thrift

Groups undertake complex development activities beyond savings and loans

Figure 4.1 Self-help versus outside support

formed without external assistance from those created or maintained with NGO or government support.

In some instances, savings groups are completely self-formed; though they may draw their inspiration from other groups or NGOs, mosques, or church groups, members self-select into groups and control their group's actions and bylaws. The first quadrant of the diagram shows that some of these savings groups are all business, engaging strictly in financial activities. For example, in two villages of rural Assam, India, households belonged on average to five savings groups, with total amounts invested of US$35. By virtue of belonging to many groups, members felt less social allegiance to each, using them for purely financial transactions (Sharma and Matthews, 2009).

The second quadrant shows that some self-engineered groups also generate their own development, with little *intentional* assistance from the outside. In the same area of rural Assam, savings groups have flourished without government or NGO assistance. Over the course of 40 years, groups in the area have transformed from weaving groups to savings groups to lucrative singing and prayer groups.

The third and fourth quadrants show that NGOs form savings groups that may take either of the previous forms. Some groups solely save and lend, while others become conduits for supplemental NGO- or government-initiated development activities. Groups in this fourth quadrant are likely the groups readers will know best. These groups are formed with outside assistance and become vehicles for aid projects, or for the distribution of commercial services.

Figure 4.1 is intended to be dynamic, its arrows suggesting that groups rarely fit discretely into one corner of a quadrant. Typically, groups are neither wholly assisted nor wholly self-forming. Few records exist for self-forming groups (quadrants one and two), so taking their census is difficult. However, some reporting is available for quadrants three and four. For example, in India, more than 7 million groups known as self-help groups (SHGs)[1] are supported by a combination of the government and 445 banks (NABARD, 2010). And the SAVIX website shows 312,000 savings groups in 60 countries, formed by an array of international NGOs.

Groups develop their members, themselves, and their communities

As discussed above, groups often form at the behest of others. NGOs might bring the concept to communities. Or, once they are trained and impassioned by their own experiences, members of savings groups may spur the creation of new circles of savers in their communities. Regardless of how groups materialize, it is clear that they can spark the development of their members and strengthen themselves as an entity – often, though not always, drawing in resources from the outside (see Chapter 3 (Rippey and Allen, 2013) for a discussion of savings group formation).

Groups develop their members

In myriad ways, savings groups usher members along a path of personal growth. Groups care for members, shame them, honor them, and occasionally dish money from a social fund to ease them out of dire straits. Let us examine just a few ways in which groups aid and develop their individual members.

Doorstep development

By the very nature of their structure, savings groups can and do provide tailored support to develop their members. Most groups have fewer than 25 members, but as many as 40 people can get to know one another well inside a few months; little time is needed for groups to know which member is doing what, and what might be ailing them. Chances are, many group members knew each other well before the group sprouted, but connect further while participating in meetings and conducing financial activities.

Using an array of carrots and sticks, groups customize support to individual members. While at times gentle healers, savings groups can also be stern purveyors of tough love, wielding threats to shape up or ship out. 'Don't accept the abuse of your spouse' and 'stop drinking' are commonly heard directives.

Consider the Birthday Officer in Porvenir, Guatemala. This is a role the group designed and established just for its member Lidia, to boost her sense of self. She reports, 'I never learned to read and write, but I have an excellent memory. I never forget a birthday.' (Andrews, 2011). These unique actions of support may spring from human kindness or from the practical need to keep members happy. After all, happy members – ones who are encouraged to take care of themselves, and encouraged in their abilities – are also loyal members, likely to protect group rules and norms.

A darker side to this kind of customization can be seen in groups pressuring members to do what they otherwise might not. For example, in Kenya members feel compelled to wear matching kangas (traditional clothing).

Dignity is development

From Colombia to Kenya, there is dignity in simple savings and lending activities. For example, Coumba from Senegal declares, 'During the first year that I belonged to a SILC group, I was like a person set free from jail. Now, I can decide what I will do with the money that I earn from the business I run' (Daouda and Sobhani, 2011). Ebenezer from Ghana reports on farming loans taken from his group, explaining that, 'This year I did not need to disgrace myself by borrowing from friends' (Asambobillah, 2011). And in Kenya, members say, 'This box holds my secrets. I now need not go from neighbour to neighbour in search of money.'

While most groups are inspired by the desire to boost savings through commitment and lending, many groups, especially those spawned by NGOs, also manage some kind of social fund which members agree to support with small but mandatory contributions. In Haiti, for example, a red box, whether real or symbolic, designates money for life-giving, emergency support for members. In Mali, special bowls or baskets divide the social fund from the internal savings and loan pool. Cash from the former is typically granted while cash from the latter is lent.

The social fund can save lives and insulate members from the shame of vulnerability in times of crisis. Members report that their special bowl or box bailed them out of medical crises (Kenya) or supplied cash to buy food (El Salvador), and in the process preserved the dignity of desperate members. Before joining a group, they would have had to hurry from neighbour to neighbour, scraping together the needed sum, or would have rushed straight into the arms of an expensive moneylender.

Household justice

Groups fight the good fight again and again, on behalf of members. They stop domestic violence and abusive dowry practices. Some shut down the sale or even use of alcohol. Others access legal and political systems that individuals would have had difficulty leveraging. In Haiti's hurricane-trampled southern peninsula, for example, a group petitioned local politicians and the court system for restitution for a young girl, the daughter of a member, who was raped by a local policeman. The group took the initiative to rally the wider community and serve as the child's legal representative in a case against a formidable system of male-dominated patronage. The officer is now in jail.

In many cases, before joining groups, women report seeing themselves as unworthy of living a life without pain; as part of a savings group, they begin to see themselves whole, particularly when groups take action on their behalf.

Groups develop themselves and their communities

Groups can be self-contained catalysts of their own development, moving beyond providing solutions for individual members in order to seize opportunities for the group as a whole. Even without outside facilitation, groups themselves can be wellsprings of change for their membership and their communities.

Do-it-yourself development

Problem-solving is critical to group evolution; without the ability to work out their own solutions, groups would be sentenced to an existence confined by the agent who formed them or the initial rules they fixed into place. Box 4.1 illustrates an example of two groups eager to improve the well-being of their membership. Drawing on their own knowledge and contacts, they pressed

---

Box 4.1 Groups as magnets for development services

In Kibera, one of Kenya's largest slums, the Gatwikera Railway Savings Club consists of 50 women and men; the club has divided them into two more manageably-sized savings groups of about 25 members each.

Minimum savings is 10 cents per day, but some members are able to coax more from their meagre incomes, depositing surpluses into their group fund. Both groups have abandoned the idea of 'the savings box', finding it a target for thieves and an inefficient way to transfer and store money. Now, they simply 'flash' their money through M-PESA into group accounts at Equity Bank. By moving their money out of the world of cash and into a digital ecosystem, groups enjoy better recordkeeping, improved methods of verification (receipts), and reduced travel and meeting time.

Tapping into the assistance of a community activist, Stanley Lukas Alube, the club has found ways to match member savings with grants and mortgages in a new housing project. Beyond daily deposits into the group fund, members each save an additional $400 over the course of more than a year. This $400 is marked for the purchase of a parcel of land located 30 kilometres from Nairobi. Muungano Wa Wana Vijiji (Kenyan Homeless People's Federation) will supplement each member's $400 with another $600 apiece to complete the sum needed for land acquisition.[2] As of December 2011, the groups had reached almost half their goal for land purchase, the first step in their process of home construction.

Housing prospects aren't the only development innovation the group initiated. To keep member spirits high, groups channel a portion of interest income toward specific member rewards. The member who saved the most received $18 (acknowledging progress), as did the member who saved the least (acknowledging perseverance).

Source: Wilson, 2011; conversations with Lukas Alube, founder of Jipange Sasa, 2011

into service a community activist, a housing NGO, a mobile money platform, and a bank.

The example in Box 4.1 highlights the variety of services a group might mobilize beyond its axial thrift and lending. True, available resources might be specific to a locale. What is within reach in Kibera might be out of reach in rural Mali; still, the principle remains the same. With creativity and common goals, groups can and do seek out services that bolster development and well-being.

Engines of faith and finance

Acquiring physical resources is not the only kind of development groups seek. In Afghanistan, for example, male members of a self-formed *itehadia* (a kind of group bank) divide meetings into three parts: the first devoted to chatting and drinking tea, the second to spiritual unity and prayer, and the third to managing money. The group sees shared expressions of its members' faith as essential to the responsible offering of financial services. Funding members' weddings is as important as funding more traditional development activities like entrepreneurship or education. This first *itehadia* sparked the creation of 11 more groups, all comprising members from the area's most marginalized tribes and religious communities (Amiry, 2010).

Many groups across Africa and Latin America combine song and prayer with group meetings. Meetings are often held in places of worship, be they churches or mosques. In South Asia most groups weave faith into finance, even if meetings seem dedicated to strictly organizational business at first glance. These expressions of faith are often spontaneous, neither engineered nor mandated by the religious institutions which may have had a hand in their formation. Members consider worship through reflection or song a mainstay of their personal and community development. If savings provides a space for meetings, and meetings provide a space for worship, then savings can indeed support this faith-based group development.

Engines of entertainment

Groups are natural drivers of entertainment for their communities. Nowhere is this more evident than with groups in Central and South America, where homegrown entertainment enlivens weekly meetings, and in some cases transforms into a profit-making venture. As collective businesses go, entertainment is a moneymaker, to the unease of some NGOs that may prefer group actions to benefit members by more traditional, asset-building standards.

In Nicaragua, for example, one savings group made far more money from hosting dances than from investing in the farm enterprises promoted by their supporting NGO. At one dance, more than 120 people arrived, including 65 men. In addition to charging for admission, the group sold beer and cigarettes on credit, collecting the money soon after the event. Earnings from the event came to $100 total, approximately $7.50 per member – well above the $2.50 average earned in local daily wages.

In some cases, entertainment is incorporated into weekly meetings. A host of Ecuadorean savings groups started by Peace Corps volunteers in 2001 draws members faithfully to every meeting with games of chance. Over time, weekly meetings have become 'microcasinos' – members purchase Bingo cards for about 25 cents per pack, and then ante up a non-monetary prize worth 50 cents. Winning members leave with prizes like rice or cooking oil, and the group profits from the sale of the cards and the antes.

While one might doubt whether frequent participation in Bingo will ultimately help build member savings, the longevity and success of this savings–entertainment formula seems promising. While legal and illegal forms of gambling are widely available in member communities, few offer the advantages of savings (Fleischer Proaño et al., 2010). This creative formula might aid in community development by offering a hybrid venue for fun and financial growth.

Engines of local income

Many groups elect to start joint ventures, with the intention of gaining a profit either to build their loan fund or to divide among members. These self-started businesses often provide valuable local services not found elsewhere in communities. Examples include shuttle services that ferry children to and from school, collective cultivation, alcohol brewing and sale, and small provision shops stocking shampoo, kerosene, fertilizer, and soap.

Collective activities seem to work best when ownership and governance are worked out well in advance. Catholic Relief Services (CRS) reports that members of a group in Mombasa, Kenya, were producing woven mats to sell in bulk. 'Tensions soon rose as some were quicker and better *makuti* weavers than others, yet received equal profit.' Piecemeal work with quality checks may have been a more appropriate form of sharing proceeds; the group might have

---

Box 4.2 Groups as enterprise

More than 500 families in one Indian village participate in a successful pickling business, an idea which sprung from savings groups. Women chop limes and tomatoes, clean tamarind, cut bittergourd, and pound chillies into pickle. Men get involved during the mango season when the fruit ripens quickly and must be processed at once.

Village women grow the ingredients or purchase them in bulk. Men transport the pickle in huge drums to distant districts, camping out for long periods to supply smaller portions to tea stalls and restaurants. During peak season, each family member hires at least ten labourers for daily wages. Per-family profit is between $800 and $1500 per year, remarkable when farming incomes in India are so low. The idea for the business was conceived in savings groups, and was nurtured for years by the entire village.

Source: EDA Rural Systems, 2006

arrived at such a solution had members thought through different approaches to production and profit-sharing.

Self-started businesses tend to develop more slowly than NGO-induced ones. Groups need time to accumulate capital and to research, test, and incubate an idea. The example in Box 4.2 is one such business that required years to mature.

Engines of justice and activism, with limits

Savings groups can and do take on many matters of social justice. They fight for peace and help members claim individual rights. They bring roads, water taps, and buses to their neighbourhoods. Some groups have staged sit-ins in front of an unjust landlord's house, held political rallies, and even launched hostile takeovers of local schools (EDA Rural Systems, 2006).

Groups cohere through actions of thrift, but take on issues that affect all residents and even visitors of a community. As the Nepal case illustrates, groups often tackle these issues of their own volition, unprompted by external influence.

NGOs offer development assistance to members, groups, and communities

In addition to the homespun examples described earlier, many NGOs feel compelled to introduce a variety of critical services that respond to the multi-dimensional challenges facing individuals, groups, and communities.

Groups as a platform for development activities

The need to assess whether savings groups and additional social, economic, and humanitarian services can complement each other reflects an old debate

---

Box 4.3 Groups as champions of activism in times of war

Marcia Odell writes of the stunning success of 288 groups that survived Nepal's political upheaval and severe human rights violations from 2001–07. All outside funding for group support had ceased by 2001, yet when their original sponsoring organization, WORTH, returned to Nepal to assess their fate, 'not only had these groups survived, but group membership had grown, from an average of 23.1 members in 2001, to 26.6 in 2007', Odell said. 'By 2007, many village bank members (savings group members) had become leaders in their communities. More than 95 per cent of the management committees said that their groups had undertaken social action of some kind. Half reported organizing local social and human rights campaigns. Responses from interviews with the committees of the 288 Village Banks revealed that groups were providing local emergency assistance, working to reduce discrimination, directing group funds toward charitable purposes, and drawing on group support to cope with the war.'

Source: Odell, 2010

in microfinance between minimalist, financial-only services, and 'integrated' services which, as the name suggests, couple the financial and non-financial. The promotion of savings groups brings this discussion to the forefront again because savings groups provide an obvious channel for innumerable and needed services. Yet, using savings groups as platforms for other services can be risky. The following are just a few examples of how NGOs have piggybacked other information, services, or products onto the existing framework of savings groups.

Survival first, development later

Some NGOs join their savings group programming with activities intended to prevent disasters from escalating into crises that threaten survival. Disaster prevention, or, as it is often called, *disaster risk reduction*, may include helping individual households reduce the risk of threats like household fires; it also includes helping entire communities to mitigate the damaging effects of recurring natural disasters, like mudslides or floods. Joint programming positions savings groups as key catalysts for such preparations.

Both sparking and nudging development

NGOs tie in various services to savings and savings groups. Services range from simple messaging to more intensive and technical interventions.

In partnership with Catholic Relief Services, Freedom from Hunger (FFH) coupled a conversation tool with savings groups in India in 2002. CRS's local partners were operating in tribal areas of several eastern Indian states

---

Box 4.4 Groups as first responders

Along the lowland coast of Odisha, one of India's poorest states, coping with crisis is the stock-in-trade of NGOs that work with savings groups. Particularly vulnerable are the families living near the banks of the Brahmani, a major river that crisscrosses plains of paddy, lentil, and coconut, watering crops and cattle, and finally emptying into the Bay of Bengal. Toward the end of the monsoon, storms threaten human life, livestock, and planted fields. Each September, tens of thousands of savings groups equip themselves for the coming floods.

A combination of government and NGO support equips groups as 'first-responders'. Members devise ways to alert each other to flood danger, from the sounding of a conch shell to the use of a mobile phone tree. Working with NGO experts, groups build boats and conduct search-and-rescue drills. Some augment their stores of food and secure them in metal bins prior to the rainiest season. Others call in loans and then disburse the group corpus (interest, fees, and principal) to members, so that all members have funds with which to shore up their homes, granaries, and livestock pens against the coming floods.

In a two-year period, one NGO saw the loss of human life in one village decrease from 104 deaths to three. Villagers owed the decrease to better preparation, facilitated in large part by the teamwork practised in savings groups.

Source: CRS, 2004

when FFH co-designed a simple product called Learning Conversations for them. Created for volunteers of church staff with limited education, Learning Conversations were conducted with groups inside fifteen-minute timeframes. These short brainstorming sessions were designed to stimulate conversation among members. After much research, FFH identified eight 'hits' where group animators could stimulate discussion along the themes of increased savings, reduced dependence on moneylenders, and ideas for simple profit-making activities. The initial set was broadened to include ideas of child protection, sustainable forestry, and the creation of grain banks.

Sometimes stronger nudges are needed to change local coping behaviours. For example, in Mali, Oxfam partners deploy field workers called 'animators' to train savings groups. As groups complete initial training on savings and lending, they become ready to receive malaria education, delivered in six sessions. Freedom from Hunger developed 30-minute 'Technical Learning Conversations' to be conducted by the animator, in which group members reflect on malaria prevention and treatment though stories, pictures, and the exchange of personal experiences with the disease. All members receive a pictorial Malaria Reminder Card, so that women can quickly recall the causes, systems, treatment, and prevention techniques discussed in the group. Evidence suggests that after participating in these conversations, group members and their families are purchasing and sleeping under insecticide-treated bed nets (AKF, 2011).

The risks of joint activity

Because SGs meet regularly to conduct their financial business, they are ideal targets for purveyors of many kinds of services; but what drives such additional services – group demand, the capacity of providers, or the whim of a donor?

In 2009 and 2010, the Aga Khan Foundation commissioned a set of case studies to explore how development organizations utilized savings groups as a springboard for other development projects. These cases examined how groups catalyzed, strengthened, or linked to services in health, agriculture, education, and marketing, and how these adjunct services created value for groups and their members. The ten case studies culminated in a paper called 'Beyond Financial Services: A Synthesis of Studies on the Integration of Savings Groups and Other Development Activities' (Rippey and Fowler, 2011). Its significant findings centre on the models for service delivery and the level of additional risk associated with added services.

Methods of delivery for joint activities

Citing a typology of integrated programmes proposed by Freedom from Hunger (Dunford, 2000), the authors summarize three basic ways in which development organizations deliver multiple services to a single community.

In the first method of joint service, *linked delivery*, two or more distinct organizations work in a coordinated fashion; one focuses on the promotion of savings groups, and the other(s) on the provision of a social service, such as housing or watershed management. In the AKF studies, linked delivery projects sought to link SGs with formal financial services, engaging a bank for this task. While this model builds on the strengths of each contributing organization, it can be challenging for the linked organizations to coordinate effectively, resulting in multiple agencies visiting a given savings group with a host of overlapping or competing services.

In the second method, *parallel delivery*, multiple staff members from the same organization provide specialized services to the same groups. For example, an expert in savings groups might gather women and men from a community and coach them through a series of savings group trainings for several months. After the group has settled into savings and lending, another staff member with expertise in agronomy, for example, might counsel members on how to improve tilling or seed storage, to be followed by a marketing specialist who helps members to fetch better prices for their farm products. Even though the experts hail from the same parent organization, their visits may also be difficult to coordinate, with complicated agendas and routes to field sites that are vulnerable to disruptions of poor roads and market days.

In the third method, *unified delivery*, one staff person delivers multiple services. For example, in Mali, field workers both train savings groups and offer malaria education. In Tanzania, the same staff member organized SGs, and later helped them to join together in agricultural marketing associations. With a single voice delivering dual messages, this method eliminates a host of coordination problems. However, it presumes that staff can be found who are able to develop expertise in multiple disciplines that are of use to SG members. The sponsoring organization must assume the costs of staff training as well as curriculum development or service design.

Highlighted in the synthesis study of the ten AKF cases (Rippey and Fowler, 2011) are a range of risks that communities face when confronting a sudden surge of services, often driven by supply. Because savings groups are so locatable and their mechanics so legible, they are perfect targets for other development services. The groups seem to have staying power too. Other kinds of development groups might unite around health or farming issues temporarily, but soon fall apart because members measure the benefits of convening against the loss and cost of time. Savings groups, however, continue to meet regularly to conduct their financial business because the financial rewards of doing so outweigh most inconveniences. Their resulting cohesiveness and predictability (i.e. meeting time and location) make them ideal targets for a range of development entities, public and private. In their synthesis of the case studies, Rippey and Fowler (2011) identify a range of risks that SGs face as a result.

Figure 4.2 plots degrees of risk along two axes. The vertical axis shows progressive financial risk to group funds. A development service would

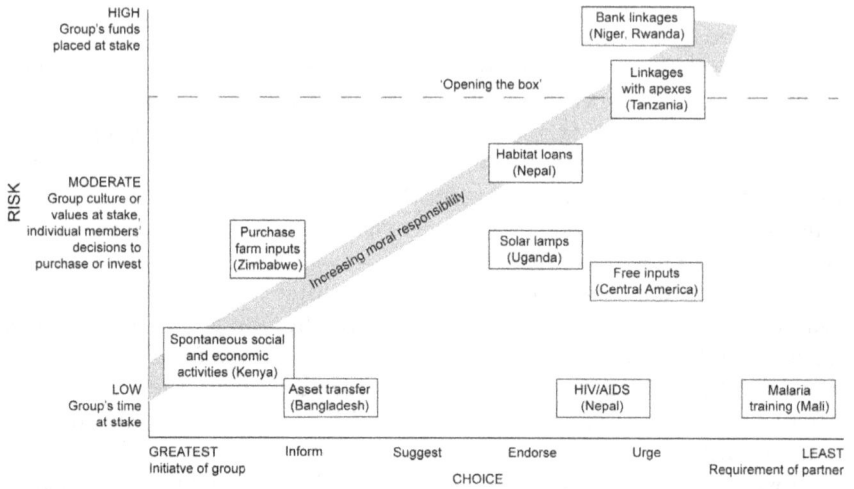

Figure 4.2 Savings group risk
Source: Rippey and Fowler, 2011

least endanger groups were it to provide information only, and not suggest or require that groups make an investment in a specific product or service. But an activity that requires investment of group funds increases risk to the group, even if those funds are matched by the development project. Group enterprises can fail no matter how carefully they are planned.

The horizontal axis measures intensiveness of forms of guidance, from passive information sharing to prescriptive instruction. Are animators simply offering information on malaria prevention and treatment, which, if conveyed properly, does not present much risk? Or are they urging groups to adopt a new farming practice, requiring an investment of capital for a technology that might produce good yields one year and catastrophic ones the next?

The solar lamp initiative in Uganda presents a case of moderate risk. Here, field staff serve as marketing agents for small solar lamps. The price of each lamp represents a lump sum difficult for rural consumers to acquire. But members of savings groups make good marketing targets because they have two options for financing their lamp purchase – they can borrow from their group or wait until share-out. In this case, the field agent is not encouraging members to 'open the box' and spend group funds; however, as a person members trust, he is encouraging individuals to spend scarce resources on a product, and enjoys a small commission on each sale.

The risks can be very real. Well-intentioned NGOs can wreak havoc on groups in this way. New groups are particularly vulnerable to the ideas and opinions of outsiders. After all, if those outsiders brought the idea of a savings group into the community, which proved so helpful, then why wouldn't all their other ideas be equally as good?

Box 4.5 Groups as targets for 'good ideas'

An NGO encouraged members of a savings group in rural Swaziland to raise chickens for profit. The women in the group were taught how to care for 'white rooster' chickens, a variety not local to the area, and less robust than the indigenous 'home' chickens. The women pooled their resources to invest in baby chicks. All of the chicks matured at the same time, and with few buyers, the local market was glutted. Members had to cut their prices by 40 per cent just to cover the cost of the baby chicks and feed. Most lost money.

Members were taught how to raise the chickens, and did as they were told. One member sighed, 'We got together and bought the chicks, but when they were ready to be eaten, no one wanted to buy them. It was a waste of chicken feed.'

Source: Zollmann, 2010

NGOs and their partners, bound by logistical frameworks and often guilty of naïveté in their initial grant-mandated assessments, may not take the time to grasp the subtleties of the real lives of the people they wish to help.

Risks to perceiving groups as targets

In 1993, an NGO in Burundi saw its savings group members become survivors of genocide. Groups reformed and continued to meet, their members still feeling the sting of slaughter. And though SG supporters posit that savings groups can be an instrument of peace and guarantors of goodwill in ethnically divided areas, one NGO leader confided that savings groups could only do so much.

Nicimpaye Dutabaran, promoter of groups under the aegis of Shigikirana Savings for Life, shares her challenges. Savings groups, she observes, tend to form along fault lines of ethnic trust. Mixed groups have difficulty bridging the suspicion and hostility perpetuated by the genocide. Asking two ethnicities with long histories of violence between them to enter into semi-permanent relationships around money seems unreasonable. As Carolyn McMahon writes of her conversation with Nicimpaye at the Arusha Savings Group Summit, 'Savings groups are not in the business of brokering deep personal forgiveness.' (McMahon, 2012). If that forgiveness emerges organically as a by-product of group membership, then that is all to the good; yet if groups gather along ethnic divides as was true in Burundi, and occurs in India's northeast or post-conflict Sri Lanka, might we imagine that these homogeneous groups could deepen the breaches between communities?

This points to a further problem. Groups are often seen as representative of communities. They are easy to find, and thus easy to herd into meetings on various topics. But, in many areas, the very poorest are not part of groups; they don't have enough to save, feel shame at attending meetings in tattered clothes, or are too engaged in the business of survival to participate in a group. With the addition of joint activities, people not part of a group face double exclusion. First, they do not receive the benefit of savings, loans, and share-outs that accompany group membership. Secondly, because they are neither easily located nor organized, they do not receive the additional services (consultations in nutrition, agriculture, malaria prevention) that may be offered through savings groups. While one could argue this might be a good thing, as the poorest would be spared possible missteps of well-intentioned NGOs, one could also argue that if the services are indeed helpful, then this exclusion could very well deepen inequities in the community.

A possible way forward: groups as co-designers

One approach to savings groups is to start them and then leave them alone, letting members and groups find their own path to development. We might call this a minimalist approach. Another approach is to start groups and continue supporting their development with additional activities until the project's natural end, typically determined by the availability of funding. We might call this a maximalist approach. A balanced approach would occupy a judicious middle ground, one that combines self-determined development with important external inputs. Arriving at that middle ground is our challenge. Perhaps a first step is for NGOs to question their pre-set formulas, rigid guidelines, and fixed offerings based on capacity, and develop an ethos of co-design.

Does it make sense for each new group to find its own way? As Julie Zollmann (2010) writes in 'Waiting for the rain, reaching for mangoes', perhaps far too much emphasis is placed on technique and far too little is placed on principles. When Zollman returned to Swaziland after being away for four years, she found that groups had little ability to innovate outside the limits that various financial and social models had imparted to them. Small variations and adaptations might have been unfolding, but, on the whole, groups were waiting for instruction from outside agencies.

A possible way forward is to support groups along their own path of discovery. Instead of viewing agents as purveyors of services, we might see them as co-explorers of a group's own development. Whether agents are volunteers or paid staff, employed by NGOs or by the groups themselves (in several variations on an emergent fee-for-service model described in Chapter 3 (Rippey and Allen, 2013)), they have a tremendous role to play in savings-led development. Agents can connect groups to local suppliers as per group interest, or gain mastery of new skills to share with members and the community. If agents are seen as agents of change and not as agents of delivery, joint development activities might square with development itself.

When groups are strong and agents good, valuable services eventually find their way into communities. Communities pull services in as needed and as available. Such patient development lies outside the typical constructs dictated by projects and funding cycles. This style of development can be seen in older groups, some which have been evolving for more than 20 years.

Box 4.6 Groups as small modern farmers

A banker on leave to complete his master's-level studies at Makere University in Kampala, Uganda, Bosco Olyeny, has not forgotten how he came to be educated. Bosco's father died when he was just three, leaving his mother to fend for herself and her children. In their home district of Apac in northern Uganda, no household has been left untouched by the violence of the Lord's Resistance Army. Many families have been driven to abandon their land and livestock.

The Apac district is relatively safe now. People are ready to farm, but fields, broken by rocks and anthills, had not been tended for years. Though some plots are up to 15 acres, farmers had been growing only modest subsistence crops. By any standard, these families remain very poor.

In 2010, Bosco returned to celebrate the December holidays in his home community. Just before Christmas, female relatives asked him to attend a savings group share-out meeting. As he sat listening to the rote counting of sums and explosions of discussion and laughter, something began to dawn on him: this was the very same group, Awak, to which his mother belonged decades ago. 'I suddenly remembered going to those meetings', Bosco said. Using group loans and dividends, Bosco's mother was able to pay for his school supplies and tuition.

While on leave from his position as manager of trade finance at the Ugandan Development Bank, Bosco realized it was time to return the kindness of his mother's group. Over the course of the past year, he pulled five savings groups together, totalling almost 200 members. Members removed stumps and stones from their fields and levelled the anthills. They rented a tractor. Bosco brought in extension workers from the government and mobilized his contacts to purchase seed and to help process and sell crops.

The land was tilled and prepared for planting. In the first season, group members harvested food to feed their families or to sell locally. Their crops included groundnuts, corn, sesame, and beans. In the second season, they farmed cotton to sell as a cash crop. The savings groups now have plans to jointly purchase a tractor, to expand their production to fruits, and to create small shops and granaries.

Source: Bosco Olyeny, interviewed at the Arusha Savings Group Summit, October 2011

Conclusion

A case could be made that adjunct services quash initiative and learning, or that they simply are not needed. An equally strong case could be made that external services bring critical support to remote areas. Unfortunately, the variety of possible add-ons, as these adjunct services are often called, is too broad to offer categorical answers to whether 'add-ons work'. No RCT or qualitative study could comprehend the manifold moving parts that constitute a pair or trio of piggybacked services. In the meantime, we are left to sort out when to bridle our social impulse to tack on more services to groups, in particular new groups that lack the defences to ward off unwanted or confusing services, and when to forge ahead, knowing groups may be the only platform onto which we might fix life-saving action and information.

For those who would appreciate the lessons drawn from both experience and research, we add wisdom noted in the paper 'Beyond Financial Services' (Rippey and Fowler, 2011).

Respect principles of good design and implementation, and good business practices

Plan carefully. Avoid creating dependency through promising handouts. Develop a clear exit strategy, and be willing to continuously make corrections.

Match delivery systems to the type of and demand for other activities

Consider which model – unified, parallel, or linked – best suits your core group product and your adjunct activity. If possible use a unified delivery model, a useful way to control costs and engender synergy between the core group product and additional programming.

Recognize additional capacity and resource requirements

Consider whether the additional activity will require redoubled training efforts or more resources. Who will bear the burden of paying for those resources? Ensure sufficient time is allowed for staff to train members on new activities, and that the additional training dovetails with seasonal realities members face.

Weigh responsibility for risk

Consider whether it is fair to put the group's own resources (its box) at stake to fund additional programme activities. Give group members the choice to participate, free from coercion; monitor results, and prepare to modify or abandon the intervention if it is not working. If necessary, indemnify group members for losses.

Separate and measure costs accurately

Develop clear, written policies for attributing costs. Consider an explicit policy that defines sustainability of core group services as well as sustainability of adjunct services.

These guidelines are relevant to organizations already forming groups and seeking to add on new social activities. With a little imagination, they can become relevant to organizations interested in introducing savings groups as adjunct services linked to current programming.

Acknowledgements

The author is grateful for comments on earlier versions received from Paul Rippey, Ben Fowler, Kathleen Stack, Megan Gash, Laura Fleischman, Alyssa Jethani, Jeffrey Ashe, marc bavois, Guy Vanmeenen, David Panetta, Eloisa Devietti, Susan Johnson, and Candace Nelson. Errors of omission or commission remain her own.

Notes

1. Self-help groups are mostly found in India. Although they are similar to the savings groups this book focuses on, they differ in important ways. See Ashe and Nelson, 2013, for a brief description of SHGs.
2. Matching funds as a supply-side policy of NGOs is not considered a best practice. But in this instance the club sought out its own matching funds.

References

Aga Khan Foundation (2011) 'Coastal Rural Support Programme, Tanzania CRSP (T): Project implementation plan agriculture and market development component 2010–2014', unpublished manuscript.

Amiry, Q. (2010) 'Chai wa paisa (Tea with money)'. Retrieved from: <http://fletcher.tufts.edu/CEME/publications/~/media/Fletcher/Microsites/CEME/newpdfs/CEME_Chai_wa_Paisa_Paper.ashx>

Ashe, J. and Nelson, C. (2013) 'Introduction', in C. Nelson (ed.), *Savings Groups at the Frontier*, pp. 1–12, Practical Action Publishing, Rugby, UK.

Andrews, S. (2011) 'The birthday officer' [blog] <http://savings-revolution.org/blog/2011/4/29/the-birthday-officer.html> (posted 29 April).

Asambobillah, R. (2011) Catholic Relief Services internal document.

Catholic Relief Services (CRS) (2004) 'Developmental relief in action: CRS-India experiences with disaster preparedness'.

Daouda, S. and Sobhani, N. (2011) CRS internal document.

Dunford C. (2000) 'The holy grail of microfinance: "helping the poor" and "sustainable"'? *Small Enterprise Development* 11(1): 40–44 <http://dx.doi.org/10.3362/0957-1329.2000.008>.

EDA Rural Systems (2006) 'Self help groups in India: A study of the lights and shades'. Retrieved from: <www.microfinancegateway.org/p/site/m/template.rc/1.9.31100/>.

Fleischer Proaño, L., Gash, M., and Kuklewicz, A. (2010) 'Strengths, weaknesses and evolution of the Peace Corps' 11-year old savings group program in Ecuador', Freedom from Hunger Research Report No. 13, Freedom From Hunger, Davis, CA.

Gash, M. (2013) 'Impact of group participation', in C. Nelson (ed.), *Savings Groups at the Frontier*, pp. 101–126, Practical Action Publishing, Rugby, UK.

McMahon, C. (2012) 'Saving a peace: How savings groups build peace', unpublished.

National Bank for Agriculture and Rural Development (NABARD) (2010) 'Status of microfinance in India: 2009–2010'. Retrieved from: <www.nabard.org/pdf/Status%20of%20Micro%20Finance%202009-10%20Eng.pdf>

Odell, M. (2010) 'Women's empowerment through literacy, banking and business: The WORTH Program in Nepal, post-program research findings', in K. Wilson, H. Harper and M. Griffith (eds) *Financial Promise for the Poor: How Groups Build Microsavings*, pp. 145–54, Kumarian Press, Sterling, VA.

Rippey, P. and Allen, H. (2013) 'Approaches to group formation', in C. Nelson (ed.), *Savings Groups at the Frontier*, pp. 65–82, Practical Action Publishing, Rugby, UK.

Rippey, P. and Fowler, B. (2011) 'Beyond financial services: A synthesis of studies on the integration of savings groups and other development activities', Aga Khan Foundation. Retrieved from: <www.akdn.org/publications/2011_akf_beyond_financial_services.pdf>

Sharma, A. and Matthews, B. (2009) 'Village financial systems in northeast India', MicroSave India Focus Note 21. Retrieved from: <www.microsave.org/briefing_notes/india-focus-note-21-village-financial-systems-in-northeast-india>

Zollmann, J. (2010) 'Waiting for the rain, reaching for mangoes: The origins, evolution, and roles of savings groups in rural Swaziland', Student Research Series, Center for Emerging Markets Enterprises, The Fletcher School, Tufts University. Retrieved from: <http://fletcher.tufts.edu/CEME/publications/~/media/Fletcher/Microsites/CEME/pubs/pdfs/Student%20Pubs%20Zollman%20Mangoes.pdf>

About the author

Kim Wilson is Senior Fellow, Center for Emerging Markets, Fletcher School, Tufts University where she is also Lecturer in Microfinance and Financial Inclusion. She consults to organizations such as CGAP and Aga Khan Foundation and has a background as a practitioner. Previously, she headed microfinance for Catholic Relief Services following a career in private-sector finance of franchiseable businesses. She is co-editor of *Financial Promise for the Poor, How Groups Build Microsavings*, published in 2010.

CHAPTER 5

Pathways to change: The impact of group participation

Megan Gash

This chapter reviews the research on the household impact of savings groups, and links the available evidence to the relative likelihood of a range of possible financial and social outcomes.

Much time and energy has been put towards understanding the impact that savings groups have on members and their families. Facilitating organizations have created and refined theories of change (TOCs) to help hypothesize the process and timeline for impacts on a member, and many studies have attempted to measure these impacts. Several studies are underway to fulfil long-term research agendas; but what does the current evidence already tell us about member- and household-level impact, and what can be gained from assessing impact at this point? A good understanding of current conclusions allows us to see which questions have been answered and which remain. As new results emerge, we can see whether new conclusions reinforce current ones, and consider how to reconcile any differences. In essence, it is valuable for the field to understand what the *entire body* of evidence on savings group impact tells us, not just one study or group of studies.[1]

This chapter summarizes the current evidence in savings group impact research by reviewing results from several studies, and identifying the likelihood that group participation creates impact in a variety of specific areas. The analysis first includes a review of key research questions and TOCs from various facilitating organizations. After taking methodological issues into consideration, the analysis identifies trends in several areas of expected impact, and ends with a discussion of what there is still to learn. The analysis is limited by the complexity of the studies reviewed; the collection spans a wide variety of programme types, timeframes, geographies, and methodological rigour. The results speak best for impacts on the most common profile studied – an adult African female who has been in a basic savings group for two years. However, great insight is also provided regarding the impacts of longer membership. The scope of studies reviewed was not exhaustive and does not include studies on traditional accumulated savings and credit associations (ASCAs), rotating savings and credit associations (ROSCAs), or the self-help group (SHG) movement in India. Overall, the current evidence suggests that while there are likely both financial and social impacts from participation, there is more impact in some areas than in others, and that length of membership is an important factor in demonstrating results.

Key research questions

What are the key questions that guide savings group impact research? What do organizations want to know? In general, questions guiding impact research focus on specific areas of expected member- and household-level impact. Most impact questions are closely linked with a facilitating organization's TOC, which is discussed in the following section. There are also often key questions not directly linked to a TOC, but that help determine whether the organization is meeting its mission – for example, whether the programme is reaching the very poor. As impact questions are answered and basic savings group programmes develop additional components, new key questions will come to the forefront.

Generalized theory of change for savings groups

Many current facilitating organizations theorize that savings groups will produce certain short-term outcomes in the first years of group partici- pation, which will lead to long-term impacts as participation continues. In this analysis, the difference between outcome and impact is somewhat an issue of time, but more so an issue of depth and magnitude. For example, a group member may use money from a loan or from accumulated savings to pay her children's school fees. The short-term outcome is that her children attend school for that year, but a long-term impact would be that her children attain higher levels of education on average (if she continues to pay the fees over time). To take another example, a group member may purchase new cookware in the first year of her membership, but go on to purchase furniture or jewellery in her third year. In the long-term, she has the capability to afford more expensive assets.

A 'generalized' theory of change for savings groups, based on those of several facilitating organizations, is included in Figure 5.1. The diagram is designed as a 'middle ground' representation of the current TOCs of several facilitating organizations. The main focus is to show the progression of inputs to impact in a generalized manner that reflects the main ideas of what many organizations currently hypothesize about savings group participation. In essence, it is a framework of general ideas.

The programme inputs in the first stage illustrated by the diagram include savings group formation, but could also include additional services provided by the facilitating organization, such as education or empowerment programmes. There is no estimated timeframe for this phase, but the assumption is that when a facilitating organization enters a community, promotes the programme, and organizes a group, the programme begins when the group starts to meet

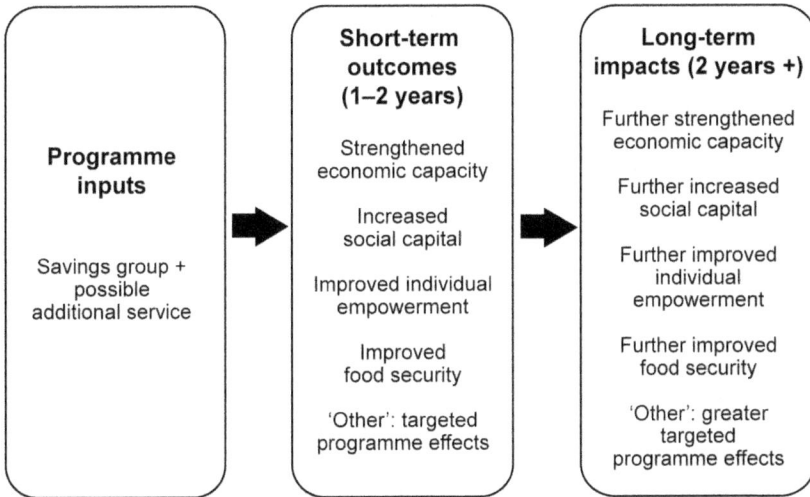

Figure 5.1 Generalized theory of change for savings groups

regularly.[2] Additional services can be offered when a group first forms, or several months later, and outcomes from that service can be anticipated at various times, depending on the type of service.

The second stage contains a list of five general domains of short-term outcomes, which should emerge within one to two years of programme participation. The Findings section of this chapter explores 14 specific areas that fall into these five domains. By domain, these areas include the following:

1. *Strengthened economic capacity*: asset accumulation, consumption-smoothing, IGA investment, management of finances, savings, and income.
2. *Increased social capital*: solidarity, collective activities, and leadership roles.
3. *Improved individual empowerment*: increased self-confidence and greater decision-making power in the household.
4. *Improved food security*: an increase in food consumption and/or a greater variation in diet.
5. *Other*: changes due to targeted programmes, such as increased specific knowledge or changes in behaviours.

The third and final stage lists long-term impacts that should appear after two or more years of participation. The list of general domains for the second stage is conceptually identical to the third, the difference being that the long-term impacts are greater and deeper manifestations of the short-term outcomes. Building upon an earlier example, a group member may first have money to pay the school fees for her children for one term or year, but as she accumulates more money (and confidence) over time, she may negotiate for more control over long-term decisions about her children's education. She may then send them to school for additional years, leading to higher levels of education for her family. Clearly, there are nuances to the long-term impacts, and Figure 5.1 intentionally only captures the general categories in which several facilitating organizations expect to see impact. Additionally, the time frame over which we can expect these impacts varies greatly depending on the domain.

A concept not included in the TOCs, but of importance to facilitating organizations, is measuring poverty levels of participants and changes in these levels over time. Poverty is a complex, multi-dimensional issue, but the intent of assigning levels is to measure poverty in economic terms. Most savings group programmes have an implied long-term goal of alleviating poverty or helping members to become wealthier, even if it is not explicitly stated in their TOCs. Some researchers try to analyse impact through indicators regarding living conditions, asset ownership, and employment opportunities; others use calibrated indices or established poverty measurement tools.[3] Although poverty-level measurement is not explicit in these TOCs, it is included in the discussion of findings here and in other chapters in this book.

A second concept not included in the TOCs is risk management, or coping mechanisms to deal with shocks. Risk management as analysed here refers to members' use of loan or savings funds in both the short term and long term to buffer their families from shocks, both foreseen and unforeseen. Some members use the funds to pay for immediate and unexpected health care or food expenses, whereas others use savings to purchase animals that they can sell at a later date when a lump sum of money is needed. Risk management is a nuanced concept that reflects the interplay of multiple domains of outcomes and impact, including economic capacity, social capital, and food security. This topic is not included as a separate domain in this analysis because none of the reviewed studies characterize findings in these terms, nor attempt to create a measure of it, although they all measured outcomes that contribute to it. It would be quite useful if future studies attempted to measure and discuss risk management in their findings, and if facilitating organizations revised TOCs to include it.

Research methods

Before examining findings from the various studies reviewed, it is important to consider how research methodology influences the validity of reported results. Much research has been done or is currently underway in the area of savings groups, but not all studies have or will produce the same results. An important question to ask is, how will we reconcile the differences? While we can easily assume that factors such as length of membership and country context explain some differences, the study design plays a less obvious, yet significant role in determining what conclusions can reasonably be made. The studies reviewed here utilize several different research designs, and it is important to keep in mind a few technical issues in order to better compare results from both past and future studies.

One significant issue to consider is the extent to which a study can prove causation, or eliminate outside factors that could otherwise explain the results. In general, impact studies try to do this by comparing the programme group with a similar group of people who do not participate in the programme, called a 'control group'. Baseline and follow-up surveys are conducted with both the programme and control groups, and results are compared.

However, control groups are often created without taking into consideration less obvious but important factors that make them different from the programme group. These differences are called selection biases, and two important ones to recognize here are *self-selection bias* and *non-random programme placement bias*. Self-selection bias refers to the inherent differences in characteristics of people who voluntarily join a programme compared to those who do not. These characteristics can make them more likely to succeed in the program – for example, volunteers may join because they already have strong savings habits or enjoy community activities. Non-random programme placement bias is the bias that occurs when villages are specifically chosen for a programme because they have characteristics that are desirable given the NGO's operational plan, such as having a high rate of low-income residents or a high degree of interest in the program (Karlan and Goldberg, 2007). Again, these characteristics can make a programme more (or less) likely to succeed in those villages.

Randomized controlled trials (RCTs), or studies with an experimental design, randomly assign villages or people to programme and control groups. Because the randomization removes self-selection bias, results coming from RCTs are often regarded as more valid and reliable than results from many other designs that do not remove these biases.[4] Non-randomized control group designs, also called quasi-experimental designs, and simple interviews or case studies, called non-experimental designs, often do not remove selection biases, and possibly create overestimated or underestimated results. Quasi-experimental evaluations with control groups can be conducted without significant biases, but they can be difficult to execute properly. Overall, both quasi-experimental and non-experimental designs are generally considered better at showing association, or correlation, than at proving causation.

A useful way to further think about the link between methodologies and their ability to prove causation is to consider where the methodology would fall on a spectrum, as shown in Figure 5.2.[5] The farther the methodology is to the right-side arrow, the better it proves causality, and the farther it is to the left-side arrow, the more it shows a non-causal association (or correlation). In general, the more rigorous the method, the more likely cause can be attributed to the intervention. Even though only a few studies included in this review prove causality, there is a valuable place for all studies in the body of evidence on savings groups. The quasi-experimental and non-experimental studies give good indications of where impact may lie, and help identify important

ASSOCIATION   CAUSALITY

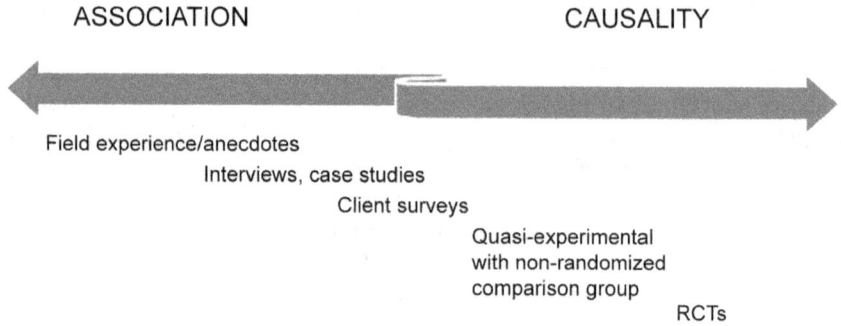

Field experience/anecdotes
         Interviews, case studies
                  Client surveys
                           Quasi-experimental
                           with non-randomized
                           comparison group
                                    RCTs

Figure 5.2 The spectrum of evidence

questions that can be more confidently answered with experimental studies. They are also more flexible in terms of identifying unanticipated impacts, and can sometimes more easily incorporate the context of the situation. Their results can also hint at explanations for results we see in experimental studies. The longer-term non-experimental studies on savings groups give us an idea of additional impacts that may emerge as participants stay in groups for longer than the one- to three-year span of some RCTs. On a practical level, quasi-experimental and non-experimental studies can be less expensive and easier to implement. We can also use quasi- and non-experimental studies, or even monitoring systems, to see whether similar results from the RCTs are showing up in other programmes. In essence, all three designs complement each other by filling in gaps and triangulating data.

Where do the studies examined in this review fall in this spectrum of evidence, and why are their positions significant? Studies included in this review fall across all parts of the spectrum (see Annex 5.1 for a description of methodologies used for the studies included in this analysis).

Some studies use one method, but many use several (or mixed) methods, for example, combining non-experimental and quasi-experimental or experimental techniques. Only a few RCTs are available to date. Overall though, the studies utilize a wide range of research methodologies and together form a balanced, impressive body of evidence on savings group impact.

Findings

This section highlights general trends in 14 areas of interest within the five domains of short-term outcomes and long-term impacts, as described in the generalized theory of change. Based on evidence presented in 15 studies, this analysis estimates a low, medium, or high likelihood that savings group participation will produce a specific outcome or positive impact in each of the 14 areas. For a list of studies reviewed to create this ranking, see Annex 5.1. As mentioned before, this analysis is not an exhaustive review of the literature available.[6] Furthermore, although many studies in this review use mixed methods to gather evidence from a variety of sources, most of the analysis focuses on the results of the quantitative survey component, which measured the member- and household-level impact.

There are several important considerations in estimating likelihood of impact. Not all the studies reviewed measured the same areas of outcomes or impact, and sometimes results were only mentioned if they reflected a positive change. Negative impacts were rarely mentioned. Therefore, it is difficult to fairly conclude that some studies found an effect when others did not. For instance, a 2010 study by DAI reported financial effects of savings groups, but did not comment on social effects; most would argue that social benefits tend to occur alongside financial benefits. That this study did not focus on social impact does not mean members gained no social benefits. Other factors considered for estimating the likelihood of impact include the dynamics of savings group functioning, how the outcome develops, interaction with other outcomes, the length of programme exposure, the type of programme, and the methodology of the research. The idea behind making these estimations is not to be highly precise or to speculate the magnitude of an effect, but simply to hypothesize about the likelihood that the outcome or impact will occur at some point during participation based on general trends found in a wide variety of studies.

Other considerations for estimation are more contextual in nature. The likelihood estimations speak for the most common situation studied: self-reported results from an African female adult participant in a savings group for approximately two years, with no or minimal additional services. Results for men were rarely mentioned, although some of the programmes evaluated did have male members. There was little variation in world region; out of the 15 studies reviewed, one was based on a programme in Nepal and another in Ecuador, but the other 13 are in west and east Africa. Eleven of the studies looked at results from six months to two years of participation, while only four included members in a programme for more than two years.

Most of the results focused on aspects one would expect from a basic savings group membership alone. Some programmes also included additional services, such as education or empowerment programmes, and results regarding those aspects are noted where relevant. Considering these contextual limitations, several studies showed similar trends and general conclusions that could be made in the 14 areas of interest.

1. Strengthening economic capacity

Asset accumulation

Asset accumulation is a very common finding among the studies reviewed, although the type of asset varies and seems related to length of membership.

In Kenya, researchers found that newer members buy inexpensive items such as wrappers (*lessos*), cooking utensils, chickens, and goats; few members were able to report a solid growth in physical assets, likely due to being in the programme for only a year (Odera and Muruka, 2007). A study in Burkina Faso looked at two cohorts of members, one in the programme for one to two years and another for two to three years, and saw some differences in their asset growth (Boyle, 2009). Many purchased both productive and non-productive assets, such as goats, sheep, poultry, agricultural inputs, utensils, storage trunks, and festival attire (dresses), but those in the older group showed more purchases of expensive items such as bicycles and jewellery. Reasons behind asset accumulation can vary, with some members buying them for immediate use and others investing in them as a long-term savings strategy (something to be sold at a later date), or even to ensure the ability to repay loans to the group in the future (BARA and IPA, 2010). It would be logical to see that as members accumulated larger savings over time, or took larger loans from a greater pool of money, they could purchase more expensive assets. Since evidence of asset accumulation was noted in several of the studies, there is a high likelihood that savings group participation will result in asset accumulation.

Consumption-smoothing

Consumption-smoothing, or the use of savings and borrowing to cover the costs of short- and long-term expenses, is the most common outcome for savings group participation for all of the studies reviewed. It is highly likely that consumption-smoothing is a short- and long-term result of savings group participation. Every study reviewed in this analysis cited that loans and/or money from distribution are used to help manage day-to-day expenses as well as plan for future purchases. Common expenses covered include foodstuffs, small household items, social activities (such as festivals and ceremonies), home repairs, education, and health care. Consumption-smoothing is closely linked with the idea of risk management as well, in that members can use loans to respond to health emergencies and food shortages, as well as cover myriad other unexpected costs.

Helping to cover the cost of education and health care is especially important because it could potentially lead to greater benefits as part of long-term impact. Many studies reported members having a perception of increased access to health care. Likely, this perceived increase did not stem from an actual increase in services available (the typical definition of access), but simply the perception that households can afford more or better services. Perhaps they feel they can seek care for an ongoing problem that they ignored before, put more money toward preventive services that they previously considered a luxury, or choose private instead of public care. A few studies mention that members greatly appreciate the reliable source of credit during emergencies, especially medical crises (Bermudez and Matuzseski, 2010), and that they see the availability of emergency loans as a form of insurance (Fleischer Proaño et al., 2010). Members potentially have a perception of increased access because they have either emergency loans or regular loans available for this purpose. They are also able to better manage personal risks with the easy access to funds and support from other members. None of the studies reviewed measured either the incidence of use or type of health care service used to see whether members accessed them more often, or accessed different ones than before programme participation. In the context of changing perceptions, how members actually cover costs and mitigate risk can be quite complex, and warrants further study.

A similar issue applies to education access or changes in school enrolment. Although members frequently reported that they used savings group money for school expenses, there was no reported change in school enrolment rates or even a change in perception of increased access to education. Allen (2009) and Allen and Hobane (2004) nevertheless noted that lack of money was no longer a reason not to send children to school. Members may be putting additional money toward health care expenses (creating an addition effect in terms of benefits), but use money from their savings group instead of money from other sources for school expenses (creating a substitution effect). Another possibility is that members are spending more money on school expenses such as buying more or better supplies (the addition effect), and just not reporting these changes. As with health care, more detailed information on how members manage such expenses would be useful to better understand these dynamics.

IGA investment

Another highly-likely result is investment in new or existing income-generating activities (IGAs). This outcome is likely in both the short- and long-term. All studies that reported on IGA investment showed an increase in new and/ or existing IGAs due to the money from loans or from accumulated savings. In Mali, women describe an increase in their small commerce activities, as well as more money invested in their commercial and agricultural activities, and claim higher returns on these investments (Bermudez and Matuszeski, 2010). However, since none of the studies reviewed reported on failed businesses, some of the 'new' activities could be efforts to reinvigorate an old business. Although IGA investment is generally a very positive outcome, this expansion or new investment can lead to other unintended and sometimes negative consequences, such as an increase in household labour, and even child labour, allocated to IGAs (Allen and Hobane, 2004; Boyle, 2009). This increase in child labour accounted for an increase in absenteeism for girls in school in Tanzania (Allen, 2009). Potentially, girls are encouraged to stay at home to either help with the IGA, or are given chores to do that the mother cannot since she is busy with the IGA. A similar situation occurred in Burkina Faso, suggesting that only when these households reach a higher level of affluence, and outside labour can be hired, can girls return to school at a level equal to that of boys (Boyle, 2009).

Management of finances and use of financial instruments

Most of the studies reviewed reported that members started to manage their personal finances differently as they gained new accounting skills and built up savings in their groups. Some of these changes pertained to better money management at home, and others involved substituting the resources accessed through the savings group for the use of other financial instruments. Women often mentioned a shift in their savings mentality, and that participation in the savings group motivated them to save more than in the previous systems they had used (BARA and IPA, 2010). Members valued the discipline imposed by the group mechanism, the ability to save for different goals, and the new culture of savings fostered in their communities (Fleischer Proaño et al., 2010). Some members use savings group loans to replace loans from other sources (Allen, 2009; Boyle, 2009). In Tanzania, Allen (2009) saw a dramatic shift in the use of savings vehicles, from family, friends, ROSCAs, and banks to savings groups. He also noted that microfinance institution (MFI) and Savings and Credit Cooperative Organization (SACCO) penetration was very low, and assumed that participants abandoned these institutions in favour of savings groups. In Zimbabwe, members reduced the use of formal sector and traditional savings instruments by 30 per cent in favour of savings group membership (Allen and Hobane, 2004). The authors attributed the change to the failure of other instruments to provide a return that compensated for the astronomical inflation, estimated at about 350 per cent per year at the time. There is a great deal of evidence suggesting that a change in the management of finances will occur with savings group membership, and will likely begin in the short term.

Savings and the creation of lump sums

Since all savings programmes require members to save, the accumulation of savings is considered a process outcome, although when members recoup these sums varies. Some groups distribute only the earned interest and put the bulk of their money back into the next cycle to build more loan capital, while others distribute the entire pot. Smaller sums received at share-out tend to go toward consumption-smoothing, and bigger sums are often used for large purchases or investments, such as furniture or significant home repairs. In Burkina Faso, researchers found that members most often invest all or part of their share-out monies in their IGAs and animals rather than spending it on school-related expenses, food for the family, or social/festive purposes (depending on the season and timing of social needs) (Boyle, 2009). As mentioned earlier, members will sometimes buy animals as a form of stored long-term savings, to sell later when they need the money quickly. In Ecuador, the sums accumulated by many members enabled them to buy furniture, pay for trips, cover Christmas expenses, and pay off other debts, such as those resulting from previously purchased appliances (Fleischer Proaño et al., 2010). Overall, these lump sums are used to smooth consumption in the short term as well as to mitigate risks in the long term. In one of the few longer-term studies, researchers found that after seven to eight years of participation, a savings group had average total assets of more than three times its holdings at the beginning, signifying that there is great potential for members to build lump sums over time (Valley Research Group and Mayoux, 2008). To understand what this potential really means, a closer look at the composition and size of the lump sums would be useful. Do members consider seven to eight years a long time to triple their money? Is the amount still relatively small compared to their overall household assets? Do members save in other ways during the savings group's cycle, and if so, what percentage of their total savings is invested in the groups? Savings groups clearly help members accumulate savings in both the short- and long-term; savings are therefore a highly likely outcome and impact, although the size and utility of the lump sum will vary per member.

Income

Most group members can likely claim an increase in income based purely on interest or dividends received at distribution, but a second and less likely aspect of the issue of increased income is whether members have invested their money in IGAs or other vehicles in such a way that it has translated into increased earnings. Only a handful of the studies cited that at least some members directly reported an increase in income, and the members usually explained that it was a result of the ability to buy more inputs with capital from loans or share-out (Abebe and H/selassie, 2009; Anyango et al., 2007; Valley Research Group and Mayoux, 2008). A few other studies infer that income has increased by observing either an increase in non-productive assets (reasoning that this indicates an increase in disposable income), or an expansion of an IGA (Allen and Hobane, 2004; Allen et al., 2010). Although these changes could be the result of increased income, a more precise look at the overall income for members and their households is necessary to confirm this. Moreover, women take repeated loans to sustain the same IGA and co-mingle IGA profits with general household income, making it unclear whether the IGA is growing or income is increasing (BARA and IPA, 2010). BARA and IPA (2010) noted that the few women they observed who have been able to realize transformative economic growth through savings group participation had enjoyed relative wealth and stability before the programme. Considering the lack of clear evidence on income growth to date, it should be assumed that this is an area of low expected impact from savings group participation, at least during the time periods studied to date (the majority of current evidence being from three to five years or less).

2. Social capital

Solidarity

The most salient area of outcomes, besides in strengthening economic capacity, is clearly in improved social capital, with the most prominent feature being that members appreciate the solidarity with other group members. Several studies mentioned how women valued the cohesion of the group as well as the friendship and support of other members. 'Social asset' strengthening among members is seen as one of the greatest achievements of a programme, and it seems to be an important motivation for participation (Odera and Muruka, 2007). It has also been suggested that the stability of the governance and leadership rules of the group added to members' social solidarity and mutual commitment (DAI, 2010). Interestingly, new members have mentioned solidarity more often than mature members as a benefit of membership (Miller and Gash, 2010). Perhaps this suggests that new members are most impressed by the group's support, but as they build on this solidarity, other benefits seem more salient. While overwhelmingly positive, the discussion of solidarity in these studies primarily comes from solidarity among women, even though the men in their lives do appreciate that it exists among them (Bermudez and Matuszeski, 2010). It would be interesting to know whether solidarity is as valuable to the male members of savings groups. Recognizing the abundance of evidence, there is a high likelihood that solidarity is an outcome of group participation for women in the short term, and it is likely they enjoy this aspect throughout their membership.

Collective activities

Since some programmes include a 'social goal', which can take the form of a collective or community-oriented activity, it is difficult to discern an increase in collective activities apart from what is expected from the group programme. Yet, it is still useful to report that a few studies noted examples of collective activities. One of the most impressive examples was from a study in Ecuador, where groups were highly active in spontaneous community activities (Fleischer Proaño et al., 2010). Most groups played bingo at weekly meetings and hosted the occasional raffle, athletic event, or dance. The members saw these activities as a way to raise money for the group and as a way to relax, have fun, build friendships, and support each other. With some older groups in Mali, savings group-based collective labour partially or wholly replaced village-wide collective labour (Bermudez and Matuszeski, 2010). The WORTH programmes in Ethiopia and Nepal, which both explicitly promote collective action, saw women working together to tackle issues that affect communities as a whole, such as harmful traditional practices, HIV/AIDS, gender-based violence, and trafficking in girls, through collective activities such as rallies and demonstrations, door-to-door campaigns, and street dramas (Abebe and H/selassie, 2009; Valley Research Group and Mayoux, 2008). Also in

Nepal, many groups also contributed to infrastructure projects such as the construction of a community building, clinic, school, library, well, or bridge, often using their own funds and sometimes attracting additional support from local government or other organizations (Valley Research Group and Mayoux, 2008). Since some of the strongest examples came from older programmes, perhaps collective activities are more likely to occur after members have built strong relationships with each other and their communities over time. It is possible that studies of mature programmes would show that collective activities prove more common among older groups. Until there is further evidence, it is safer to estimate that there is a medium likelihood that savings group programmes will create this outcome.

Leadership roles

Another expected outcome is for women to take on leadership roles in community activities. Some women gain confidence and experience from participating in the management committee of their group and become leaders in other community groups, whereas others who were already in those roles in other groups bring these experiences to savings groups. A typical example of the former when women who previously had only worked in their homes or fields, then go on to become group presidents, replicating agents, or representatives at commune-level associations (Bermudez and Matuszeski, 2010). In Burundi, nearly one-half of members surveyed held administrative positions in community groups (Allen et al., 2010), and in Zimbabwe, accession to leadership or committee membership in additional groups increased by 77 per cent (Allen and Hobane, 2004). Another study also saw participation in management committees improve leadership skills of women, with the majority holding leadership positions in other community groups, churches, and welfare associations (Odera and Muruka, 2007). Furthermore, many studies observed gains in levels of respect and status within their households and the wider community, which, when appreciated by others, likely gave them the confidence and ability to become leaders in other areas. Although there are some good examples of the transference and development of leadership skills, it is not clear in the evidence reviewed that this is a very common occurrence, and therefore there is only a medium likelihood that it will occur. A partial explanation may be found in the limited number of leadership positions available to women in communities where savings group programmes work, but it is likely that some women, and not all group members, gain or develop these skills.

3. Individual empowerment

Self-confidence

The studies reviewed often addressed issues of empowerment differently, with some commenting on self-confidence and self-respect and others on increased independence or mobility. The strongest outcomes came from the studies of older groups. Bermudez and Matuszeski (2010) found several outcomes related to self-confidence. They found that the Malian women from mature groups had a new prominence within their households and communities and expressed pride, which sometimes translated into an improvement of their personal appearance and in turn their self-respect. The authors noted that many group members exhibited increased ambition and drive through their various projects and goals (such as soap-making, shea butter production, cloth dyeing, and mill work), and exhibited an avid interest in learning new business skills and exchanging ideas with other group members. A study on mature groups in Nepal found that respondents said the programme had helped give their work greater recognition in the community, increased mobility, increased their self-confidence, and strengthened their ability to make decisions (Valley Research Group and Mayoux, 2008). Experience with public speaking led to more confidence for various members as well (Valley Research Group and Mayoux, 2008 and Fleischer Proaño et al., 2010). Outside of these positive outcomes, a study of groups two to three years old found no clear significant difference regarding self-confidence (Boyle, 2009). This finding indicates that changes in self-confidence become most evident after a minimum of three years of participation, and are considered as having a higher likelihood of occurring in the long-term rather than the short-term. Overall, there is a medium likelihood of seeing increases in self-confidence.

Decision-making power in the household

A fair number of studies claimed an increase in women's decision-making power in the household. Most frequently, a woman's newfound ability to make decisions about her own IGA demonstrated an increase in decision-making power, but it also manifested in a greater ability to make decisions about the affairs of her children and management of household expenses. Men appreciated the women's confidence and ability to manage finances and care for their children (BARA and IPA, 2010), and a gain in decision-making power may come about by this appreciation of the increased contributions from women, possibly including their increased access to loans (Bermudez and Matuszeski, 2010). The increase in decision-making power often seems to be represented by an increase in joint decision-making between the husband and wife, which can lead to improved marital relationships (Allen and Hobane, 2004; Bermudez and Matuszeski, 2010). Increases in decision-making power can occur regarding children's marriages, buying and selling household properties, sending children to school, attending public meetings, and family planning (Abebe and H/selassie, 2009). Some women even became sole decision-makers in place of their husbands (Valley Research Group and Mayoux, 2008). Despite these reports, Allen et al. (2010) found no significant impact on empowering women to have more control over household decisions, and hypothesizes that female empowerment at the household level tends to emerge when the economic impact becomes clear, usually after two-and-a-half to three years (the 2010 study looked at participants with two years of participation). This hypothesis is in line with findings in Burkina Faso, in which control over a woman's IGA was higher for those in the programme for two to three years than for those in the programme for one to two years (Boyle, 2009). Recognizing the mixed outcomes in this area, it is estimated there is a medium likelihood that savings group participation results in increased decision-making power in the household.

4. Food security

Some studies showed positive outcomes for food security, especially increased consumption and/or a more varied diet (but not in terms of access to and utilization of food, as food security is traditionally measured). This finding makes sense in light of strong outcomes reported for consumption-smoothing. A study in Burundi showed members eating comparably 20 per cent more per day and having substantially higher food stocks (Allen et al., 2010). Other studies found increased consumption and increased variety of all food types (Allen and Hobane, 2004; Bermudez and Matuszeski, 2010). In Burkina Faso, a researcher found greater consumption and variety in foods for all members in his study, but found greater food security for women in the programme for three years as opposed to those in the programme for two years (Boyle, 2009). Similarly, a study in Mali found that many women in the programme for more than two years scored as more food-secure than newer members on a food-security scale, although a high percentage of both newer and mature members scored as food-insecure overall (Miller and Gash, 2010). As with several other outcomes, results for food security seem to be affected by membership length. There could be various reasons to explain a greater stability in food security over time, such as more consistently available cash to buy food and an increased ability to grow more food due to investment in an agriculturally-oriented IGA, or learning from other members about better methods of growing crops. Although there is evidence to suggest increases in food availability, more evidence would be helpful to demonstrate whether members and their families eat regularly, share food throughout the entire household, and worry less about its availability. Recognizing these aspects, greater food security is considered a somewhat (or medium) likely outcome from participation.

5. 'Other' or outcomes from additional services

About half of the savings group programmes examined either included additional services, such as health education, or were components added to other non-savings programmes (e.g. assistance for displaced people or those living with HIV/AIDS). Some of the studies looked at indicators specific to the 'other' programme, and only a few of them set up a design in which the savings group alone could be compared against the savings group with the additional service. Therefore, it is difficult to understand which effects are due only to the additional service or only to the savings group. Additionally, even though the effectiveness of the non-savings programme likely has much to do with its own inputs, it is possible that already-existent group solidarity enhances the effectiveness of the non-savings programme. For instance, it could be easier for members to talk about domestic violence through a dialogue series (i.e., the additional or 'other' programme) if the members already feel comfortable and trust each other through a bond they formed by saving and managing finances together. Due to the great variability in both programme inputs and services provided, the concept of outcomes from additional services was not included in the likelihood-ranking exercise.

Nevertheless, it is useful to know that many of these additional services showed strong outcomes. Annan et al. (2011) found that although child well-being increased in Village Savings and Loan Associations (VSLAs), the increase was greater in VSLAs paired with a family-based discussion group series (introduced by the International Rescue Committee) that addressed risks for children who are returned refugees to Burundi. Participation in savings groups and the discussion series reduced harsh physical and verbal discipline at home, reduced the incidence of family problems, and improved the mental health of children whose caretakers participated in VSLAs and the discussion series. The PACT WORTH women's empowerment and literacy programmes in Nepal and Ethiopia resulted in changes in women's ability to deal with domestic violence and in helping women learn to read, change their attitudes about literacy education, and, specifically in Ethiopia, increase the number of children sent to school (Abebe and H/selassie, 2009; Valley Research Group and Mayoux, 2008). A World Relief HIV and AIDS care and prevention programme, coupled with a savings group programme, resulted in having more family members tested for HIV, more of their children aware of the ways of transmitting HIV, and an increase in groups that have reached out to provide support to community members with HIV/AIDS (Allen et al., 2010). Although we have yet to see a study that closely compares the effectiveness of integrating these types of programme into savings groups as opposed to another type of financial service group, overall it seems that savings groups can be an effective platform for delivering additional services.

Poverty-level measurement

In the studies reviewed, there is very little evidence that participation in savings groups has clearly changed the poverty levels of members (as measured through the established aforementioned indices). The one study that does show gains in this area was with savings groups of returned refugees in Burundi. Annan et al. (2011) found that participation in savings groups seemed to have helped households avoid a downward economic trend in rural Burundi, resulting in a net impact of a 14 per cent reduction in the number of families living below the poverty line (proving to be statistically significant). This finding is striking, and is especially meaningful because it is a change that can be confidently attributed to programme participation due to the experimental design of the study.

Unfortunately, none of the studies in this review, which include mature or longer-term programmes, had a baseline that included a solid measurement of poverty levels of participants. Studies in Nepal and Ecuador noted that many current members may have been poor but were not among the poorest, and it is unclear whether a change in poverty level occurred during participation in the programme. There is evidence that savings groups can and do include and attract the very poor, but it is important to note that they also appeal to the not-very-poor. Outreach to the poor is further explored in other chapters of this book. Moreover, asset accumulation and increases in income could eventually lead to changes in poverty level, but, at this point, there are no programmes reporting clear economic transformation for poor members.

Summary

Overall, we can speculate that savings group participation is welfare-enhancing through the creation of both financial and social benefits, with impacts being stronger in some areas than others. Figure 5.3 illustrates the relative likelihood of the various possible outcomes.

There are a few exceptions to note. Even though changes in the rate of school enrolment were not treated as a separate result in the Findings section of this chapter, they are included in the TOCs of multiple facilitating organizations, and therefore needed to be assessed in terms of the likelihood of occurrence.

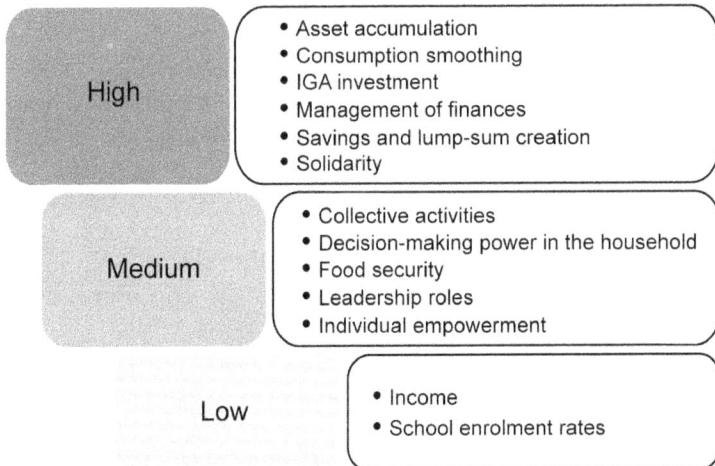

High
- Asset accumulation
- Consumption smoothing
- IGA investment
- Management of finances
- Savings and lump-sum creation
- Solidarity

Medium
- Collective activities
- Decision-making power in the household
- Food security
- Leadership roles
- Individual empowerment

Low
- Income
- School enrolment rates

Figure 5.3 Likelihood of expected member and household-level impacts for SG participation

Changes in poverty levels and risk management are not included in Figure 5.3. The studies reviewed did not provide enough explicit information on these two concepts to make a fair assessment. One could speculate, though, that there would be a high to medium likelihood that risk management would occur (and is both a short- and long-term impact). Changes in poverty level could occur, especially as seen in the case of returned refugees, but most likely it is a long-term impact for most members. Additionally, the category of 'other' for additional services is not included in this ranking since the likelihood of impact depends greatly upon the service delivered, and does not speak to the outcomes for basic savings group participation (since the additional service extends beyond what is 'basic'). The only area of potentially negative impact presented in the studies is in regards to IGA investment leading to increased absenteeism in school for girls. Since this was only noted in two studies (and needs further exploration), it is also not included in Figure 5.3.

An important nuance, often mentioned throughout the Findings, is *when* these outcomes and impacts occur. Since this analysis attempts to best capture what the 15 studies have reported, it is not possible to adequately map out when each of the outcomes and impacts should occur because important details are lacking, as are more long-term studies. However, based on some of the data, in combination with field observations, we can speculate when some of these outcomes and impacts would occur. Whereas Figure 5.3 summarizes the likelihood that the outcomes in question will present themselves *at any point* during savings group participation based on these studies, one could speculate that the following impacts would occur along the following timelines.

For one to two years of programme participation:

- Small-asset accumulation, consumption-smoothing, IGA investment, management of finances, savings and lump-sum creation, solidarity among members, food security, and risk management.

For two to three years and more of participation:

- Large/expensive-asset accumulation, continued consumption-smoothing, further IGA investment (potentially more new business investment), further and continued management of finance, greater savings and better lump-sum creation, increased solidarity, further risk management, collective activities, greater decision-making power in the household, greater food security, leadership roles, individual empowerment, greater income (although only likely for a minority), and changes in poverty levels (although probably more likely in the very long term of five to ten years).

Still to learn

Current evidence to date has shown that we can hypothesize about several areas of expected short-term outcomes and long-term impacts. However, gaps remain in those areas, and some level of uncertainty remains due to the inability of the research designs to confidently attribute results to the programmes. Considering these issues, what is there still to learn? Some of the unanswered questions include: Are members accessing health care services more often because they now feel they are more affordable? Are girls' enrolment rates truly dropping with the expansion of IGAs? Are members using loans and accumulated savings to pay for new expenses (creating an addition effect), or substituting these funds for money from other sources such as family, friends, or a ROSCA? If women's IGAs are expanding, are they bringing in more profit? Addressing these nuances will further verify the TOCs of several facilitating organizations.

What about wider questions that tie some of these outcomes together? For instance, at the Arusha Savings Group Summit in 2011, Stuart Rutherford posed the following questions about the utility of savings groups as a financial tool for the poor: How well do savings groups help the poor manage day-to-day finances? How well do they motivate them to save, and to accumulate lump sums for both expected and unexpected events? Rutherford stated that he thought savings groups help motivate members to save and help somewhat with managing day-to-day finances, but the question about the accumulation of lump sums still remains. Considering these issues, do facilitating organizations feel satisfied with the ways that savings group participation helps members with financial management, or are there some tweaks that can be added to make them more effective?

In addition to these concepts, new trends in savings group services bring up new questions about member- and household-level impact. Some questions emerging about new innovations include:

- What is the impact of additional services, such as financial education or empowerment programmes, on members?
- What is the impact of participation for youth who form savings groups of their own?
- What is the impact on individual members of linking with formal financial services?
- How do the delivery channels, such as the private service provider or the village agent models, affect the magnitude of member- and household-level impacts?
- What are the differences in impact of programmes in different geographic areas?

Studies scheduled to conclude in 2012 and 2013 may answer some of the questions raised by the current evidence and speak to some of the emergent issues. Although some of these studies have baseline data available, most (with the exception of the midterm outcomes from the IRC study) were not included in this analysis of current evidence because they did not speak clearly to observed impacts. Studies with data publicly available at the time of this analysis are listed in Table 5.1.

Table 5.1 Ongoing savings group studies

Organization	Type of programme	Country	Evaluator	Methodology and projected end date
CARE	VSLA	Multiple; across Africa	NGO	Quarterly client survey (includes poverty date); ongoing system
CARE	VSLA	Uganda, Malawi and Ghana	Third party	Experimental; end date 2011; data available in early 2012
CRS	Savings and internal lending communities (SILC)	Kenya, Uganda and Tanzania	Third party	Experimental; compares private service provider to field agent delivery channels; two-year study, end date 2012
IRC	VSLA and discussion series	Burundi	Third party	Experimental; end date 2012, midterm data available now
Oxfam America and Freedom from Hunger	*Saving for Change* and malaria education	Mali	Third party	Mixed methods with experimental quantitative survey, financial diaries, and quasi-experimental qualitative component; end date 2012
Oxfam America	*Saving for Change*	Cambodia	Third party	Mixed methods with quasi-experimental quantitative survey; end date 2012; baseline data available
Oxfam America	*Saving for Change*	Guatemala	Third party	Mixed methods with quasi-experimental quantitative survey; end date 2012; baseline data available

Source: publicly available data, 2012

In addition to these studies, some facilitating organizations have learning agendas that will explore additional topics. Financial Sector Deepening (FSD) Kenya has an extensive research agenda for the coming two years that includes a cost-effectiveness study (involving CARE, Catholic Relief Services, and the Aga Khan Foundation), a poverty census study, a study of marginalized areas, an impact study of savings groups at the meso or community level, a major comparative study of delivery models that looks at cost as well as quality, and a financial diaries study to help examine a financial education component for savings groups. In addition, the Aga Khan Foundation plans to collect member surveys across multiple countries in South Asia, Central Asia, and East Africa, and World Vision Canada is conducting a study in East Africa with an emphasis on child well-being. Between the current evidence and these ongoing and future studies, the short-term impact of savings group participation will be increasingly well understood and documented.

Conclusion

This review has created solid hypotheses on the likelihood of expected member- and household-level impact, and allows us to better understand where future research results will fit into the body of evidence on savings group impact. The domains with the strongest likelihood of demonstrating impact are financial and social – namely, strengthened economic capacity and increased social capital. As stated earlier, there is a high likelihood of positive impact in the following areas: asset accumulation, consumption-smoothing, IGA investment, management of finances, savings and lump-sum creation, and solidarity with other members. The areas with a medium or fair expectation to show impact are collective activities, decision-making power in the household, self-empowerment, food security, and leadership roles. And lastly, the areas with a low expectation of impact are in income and school enrolment rates. We can speculate that there is a medium-to-high likelihood of impact in risk management, although it is still difficult to say whether there will be changes in members' poverty levels. The type and context of the studies in this review vary greatly, but the general conclusions drawn from them should hold true for basic savings groups in a variety of settings.

There is, of course, more to learn. Further explanation is needed to understand the nuances of financial and social benefits. For instance, what do impacts add up to in a member's life? How are her perceptions and attitudes changed? If poverty alleviation is the end goal of savings groups, to what extent do these impacts contribute to that goal? Questions also remain regarding regional differences, how useful savings groups are as a financial tool for the poor, and how various additional services and financial linkages modify impact. Upcoming research will speak to some of these issues, and the outcomes will need to be considered alongside what the body of evidence tells us thus far. The review of studies in this chapter sets up a framework for this comparison. Additionally, the generalized theory of change, coupled with insight from older groups, gives us a foundation upon which to shape future thinking about savings groups, and what impacts can be expected with continuous participation. Understanding these long-term impacts may be the key to finding out whether savings groups are the agents of change they are hoped to be.

Acknowledgements

The author would like to express her gratitude to the following individuals for either sharing materials that contributed to the content of the chapter or for insightful and helpful comments on earlier versions, or both: Jeffrey Ashe, marc bavois, Sybil Chidiac, Eloisa Devietti, Chris Dunford, Mike Ferguson, Laura Fleischer Proaño, Amrik Heyer, Alyssa Jethani, Susan Johnson, Joanna Ledgerwood, Clelia Anna Mannino, Janina Matuszeski, Candace Nelson, David Panetta, Paul Rippey, Wendy Sinnema, Bram Thuysbaert, Pieter Vandermeer, Sarah J. Ward, Kim Wilson, and Kathy Younker.

Notes

1. This reiterates the point that Kathleen Odell made in 'Measuring the impact of microfinance: Taking another look' (2011). She reconciles differences in outcomes from several studies of varying rigour on microfinance.
2. It is important to note that the short-term outcomes and long-term impacts discussed should not be confused with process outcomes, which do not tell us about effects resulting from the programme but rather describe outputs, such as the number of savings groups formed or the number of women reached.
3. The most common tools used in the field of financial inclusion are the Progress Out of Poverty Index™ <http://progressoutofpoverty.org/> and the USAID Poverty Assessment Tool <www.povertytools.org>.
4. Although this view is widely accepted in multiple disciplines within social science and other scientific research, it is important to note that some researchers disagree with it.
5. The 'Spectrum of Evidence' is courtesy of Kathleen Odell, Assistant Professor of Economics, Brennan School of Business, Dominican University. Presentation at the Global Microcredit Summit, November 2011, from the workshop, 'The debate on outreach and impact of microfinance: What do we know and how do we know it?'
6   Selection of studies included depended on prominence of the study to the field, availability to the author, prior knowledge of the study to the author, requests by facilitating organizations to be included, and availability of analysed data that could be shared publicly. Some studies, such as Anyango et al. (2007), were included because they were well-known in the field and provided valuable insight, although they are not impact assessments per se.

References

Abebe, S. and H/selassie, B. (2009) 'Report on impact evaluation of WORTH literacy-led saving and credit program', Pact Ethiopia, Addis Ababa.

Allen, H. (2009) 'Impact and programme evaluation of Plan and UHIKI's joint VSL programme in Tanzania', VSL Associates, Solingen, Germany.

Allen, H. and Hobane, P. (2004) 'Trip report: Impact evaluation of Kupfuma Ishungu', CARE, Harare and Arusha.

Allen, H., Panetta, D., and Stokes, S. (2010) 'Impact evaluation report of Shigikirana: Savings for Life', The Baptist Union of Denmark, Dutabarane and World Relief, Burundi, and VSL Associates, Solingen.

Annan, J., Armstrong, M., and Bundervoet, T. (2011) 'Urwaruka Rushasha: A randomized impact evaluation of village savings and loans associations and family-based interventions in Burundi', Evaluation Brief, International Rescue Committee, New York. Retrieved from: <www.rescue.org/sites/default/files/resource-file/new%20generation%20brief_%20midterm%20with%20cover_FINALJan%2027.pdf>

Anyango, E., Esipisu, E., Opoku, L., Johnson, S., Malkamaki, M. and Musoke, C. (2007) 'Village savings and loan associations: Experience from Zanzibar' *Small Enterprise Development* 18(1):11–24.

Bermudez, L. and Matuszeski, J. (2010) 'Ensuring continued success: Saving for Change in older program areas of Mali', Oxfam America, Boston, MA.

Boyle, P. (2009) 'Evaluation of impact of the Tougouri Pilot Project and establishment of baseline data for phase II', Namentenga Village Savings & Loan Project, Plan Burkina Faso.

Bureau of Applied Research in Anthropology (BARA) and Innovations for Poverty Action (IPA) (2010) 'Baseline study of Saving for Change in Mali: Results from the Segou Expansion Zone and existing SfC sites', University of Arizona, Tucson. Retrieved from: <www.ffhtechnical.org/resources/articles/baseline-study-saving-change-mali-results-segou-expansion-zone-and-existing-sfc-s>

DAI (2010) 'Group savings and loans associations: Impact study', FSD Kenya. Retrieved from: <www.fsdkenya.org/pdf_documents/11-01-19_GSL_Impact_assessment_study.pdf>

Fleischer Proaño, L., Gash, M., and Kuklewicz, A. (2010) 'Strengths, weaknesses and evolution of the Peace Corps' 11-year old savings group program in Ecuador', Freedom from Hunger Research Report No. 13, Freedom From Hunger, Davis, CA.

Karlan, D. and Goldberg, N. (2007) *Impact Evaluation for Microfinance: Review of Methodological Issue,* Doing Impact Evaluation No. 7, The World Bank, Washington, D.C.

Miller, J. and Gash, M. (2010) 'Saving for Change impact stories research: Extended report', FFH, Davis, CA. Retrieved from: <www.ffhtechnical.org/resources/research-reports/isaving-changei-impact-stories>

Odell, K. (2011) 'Measuring the impact of microfinance: Taking another look', Grameen Foundation Publication Series, Washington, D.C. Retrieved from: <www.grameenfoundation.org/measuring-impact-microfinance-taking-another-look-0>

Odera, R. and Muruka, G. (2007) 'Savings and internal lending communities (SILC) in Kenya: Program review', MicroSave. Retrieved from: <www.microsave.org/sites/default/files/research_papers/SILC%20Program%20Review%20Kenya%20December%202007.pdf>

Valley Research Group and Mayoux, L. (2008) *Women Ending Poverty: The WORTH Program in Nepal: Empowerment through Literacy, Banking and Business 1999–2007*. Retrieved from: <www.pactworld.org/galleries/worth-files/Nepal_Final_Report_Letter_0825_PDF.pdf>

About the author

Megan Gash joined Freedom from Hunger in 2007. She works with partner organizations to design, implement, and analyze research and evaluation studies that measure the efficacy of their programmes. She also provides relationship management with local and international research institutions, consultants, and interns involved with Freedom from Hunger research initiatives. Before joining the organization, Megan worked in microfinance research with a focus on poverty assessment, and conducted trainings and carried out field research in Central America, east Africa, and Southeast Asia.

Annex 5.1 Review of savings group studies

Author and study title	Country	Organization	Type of programme	Average length length of time in programme as of report	Type of evaluator	Methodology of study
Abebe and H/selassie, 2009: *Report on Impact Evaluation of WORTH Literacy-led Savings and Credit Program*	Ethiopia	PACT Ethiopia	Savings groups; WORTH literacy, business training and collective action programme	2 years	Third party	Mixed methods with non-experimental quantitative survey
Allen, 2009: *Impact and Programme Evaluation of Plan and UHIKI's Joint VSL program in Tanzania*	Tanzania	Plan Tanzania	VSLA	1–2 years	Third party	Mixed methods with quasi-experimental quantitative survey
Allen and Hobane, 2004: *Impact Evaluation of Kupfuma Ishungu*	Zimbabwe	CARE	VSLs	2–4 years	Third party	Mixed methods with quasi-experimental survey quantitative
Allen et al., 2010: *Impact Evaluation of Shigikirana Savings for Life*	Burundi	World Relief	VSLA; HIV/AIDS care and prevention programme	2 years	Third party	Mixed methods with quasi-experimental quantitative survey
Annan et al., 2011: *Urwaruka Rushasha: A Randomized Impact Evaluation of Village Savings and Loans Associations and Family-Based Interventions in Burundi*[1]	Burundi	IRC	VSLA; Healing Families and Communities discussion series	1 year	Third party	Experimental
Anyango et al., 2007: *Village Savings and Loan Associations – Experience from Zanzibar*	Tanzania (Zanzibar)	CARE	VSLAs	2 years	Third party	Mixed methods with quasi-experimental quantitative survey
BARA and IPA, 2010: *Baseline Study of Saving for Change in Mali: Results from the Segou Expansion Zone and Existing SfC Sites*[1]	Mali	Saving for Change	Malaria education	2–4 years	Third party	Mixed methods with experimental quantitative survey and quasi-experimental qualitative component

Author and study title	Country	Organization	Type of programme	Average length length of time in programme as of report	Type of evaluator	Methodology of study
Bermudez and Matuszeski, 2010: Ensuring Continued Success: Saving for Change in Older Program Areas of Mali	Mali	Oxfam America, Saving for Change	Malaria education	3–4 years	NGO and consultant	Mixed methods with quasi-experimental quantitative survey
Boyle, 2009: Evaluation of Impact of the Tougouri Pilot Project and Establishment of Baseline Data for Phase II	Burkina Faso	Plan Burkina Faso	VSLAs	Cohort 1: 1–2 years; cohort 2: 2–3 years	Third party	Mixed methods with quasi-experimental quantitative survey
Brannen, 2010: An Impact Study of the Village Savings and Loan Association (VSLA) Program in Zanzibar, Tanzania	Tanzania (Zanzibar)	CARE	VSLs	5 years	Third party	Mixed methods with quasi-experimental quantitative survey
DAI, 2010: Group Savings and Loans Associations Impact Study	Kenya	FSDKenya; CARE Group	Savings and Loan programme (some financial literacy training included)	2 years	Third party	Mixed methods with quasi-experimental quantitative survey
Miller and Gash, 2010: Saving for Change Impact Stories Research Extended Report	Mali	Freedom from Hunger; Saving for Change	Malaria education	6 months – 2 years	NGO and consultant	Non-experimental
Odera and Muruka, 2007: Savings and Internal Lending Communities (SILC) in Kenya: Program Review	Kenya	CRS; SILC (as part of APHIA II, OVC PEPFAR and The Children Behind (TCB))	HIV/AIDS programmes	1 year	Third party	Non-experimental
Fleischer-Proaño et al., 2010: Strengths, Weaknesses and Evolution of the Peace Corps' 11-Year-Old Savings Group Program in Ecuador	Ecuador	Peace Corps Ecuador	Savings groups	3–11 years	Third party	Mixed methods with non-experimental quantitative survey
Valley and Mayoux, 2008: Women Ending Poverty: The WORTH Program in Nepal	Nepal	PACT Nepal	Savings groups; WORTH literacy, business training and collective action programme	7 years	Third party	Mixed methods with quasi-experimental quantitative survey

[1] ongoing study; end date 2012

CHAPTER 6

Performance monitoring

David Panetta

This chapter reviews the management information systems that focus on the financial performance of savings groups and the efficiency of the agencies that promote them. The Aga Khan Foundation, Catholic Relief Services, CARE, and Oxfam systems are examined in light of the standard VSL MIS.

The external evaluator entered the room, and the programme manager directed his attention to the contents of a dusty filing cabinet. 'These are all the monthly records of every savings group since the inception of the programme,' the programme manager explained proudly, pointing to thousands of records.

> 'And how is this data processed?' asked the evaluator.
> 'Processed?' enquired the programme manager.
> 'Yes,' answered the evaluator. 'How are these records analysed, and for what purpose?'
> 'These records are kept here and are always available to any stakeholder,' explained the programme manager.
> 'Which stakeholders?' asked the evaluator.
> 'Anyone who is interested,' answered the programme manager, removing numerous boxes of age-stained surveys from behind a row of broken bicycles.

Perspectives on performance monitoring: does it matter and for whom?

The value of any monitoring system must be measured against the usefulness of the actionable information it generates for stakeholders, and the costs – financial and non-financial – of developing and maintaining the system.

There are three main stakeholders in the performance monitoring of savings groups: donors, programme management, and the groups themselves. The primary interests of donors and implementing agencies are to track the overall progress of their investments, to measure the returns of these investments against expected outcomes, and to use that experience to improve future programme design and funding decisions. Active performance monitoring enables programme managers and supervisors to manage resources – particularly their time – more strategically. And finally, the focused performance monitoring of savings groups enables programme staff to identify weaknesses and correct them through more targeted training and supervision, ultimately improving the groups' safety, operating efficiency, and financial performance.

A useful performance monitoring system must collect, store, and process actionable information to meet the needs of its stakeholders. For the system to be viable, it must accomplish these tasks at a reasonable cost, without creating an overwhelming burden on practitioners and groups.

A standardized management information system: tools, requirements, outputs, and stakeholders

The primary performance monitoring tool used by agencies that promote savings groups is the VSL Management Information System. The open-source software is an Excel-based, standalone MIS solution for agencies that promote savings groups. The system is an effective reporting tool for donors and implementing agencies and, moreover, it enables programme management to identify differences in performance across programme areas, staff, and groups.

The VSL Management Information System was developed by VSL Associates with support from the Bill & Melinda Gates Foundation, CARE, Catholic Relief Services, Oxfam America, and Plan International. The adoption of a common management information system by most of the agencies that promote savings groups worldwide has advanced the standardization of reporting in the sector, and has enabled all practitioners and donors to adopt a standalone MIS solution that might otherwise be prohibitively costly and time-consuming to develop separately.

Structure and reports

The VSL Management Information System is structured around four primary reports:

1. *Performance Ratios*. The overall Performance Ratios report provides a concise overview of the programme based on a selection of 16 key performance indicators developed by the Savings-Led Financial Services Working Group of the SEEP Network.[1] All monetary figures are presented in the local currency as well as in an external reporting currency defined by the user. This report enables external audiences to assess the overall performance of the programme and compare results across programmes and other microfinance initiatives, mainly using standardized metrics from the microfinance sector.

2. *Overall Project Performance*. The Overall Project Performance report provides a detailed summary of the programme's progress based on 48 metrics, which cover the programme's outreach, the profile of group membership, the groups' financial performance, and the operational and financial efficiency of the implementing agency. This report enables programme management to monitor the overall performance and track progress toward outreach and budgetary targets. For example, a sudden change in the savings mobilization rate may alert programme

management to changes in member confidence, or to external factors such as economic or seasonal cycles that influence the savings capacity of members in the programme area.

3. *Portfolio Performance Comparison.* The Comparison report provides the consolidated portfolio performance data of each trainer based on 13 key performance indicators. In expanding and medium-to-large-scale programmes, this report is perhaps the most important management tool. It helps identify differences in performance across trainers, allowing programme management to allocate resources and efforts more efficiently and resolve weaknesses that would otherwise remain unnoticed for longer periods. For example, a trainer with a member dropout rate that is considerably greater than the programme average deserves immediate and additional supervision by programme management. The Portfolio Comparison Report would identify this need more promptly than casual supervision alone.

4. *Field Officer Portfolio Analysis.* The Field Officer report summarizes the position of each group in the portfolio of the selected trainer. The report includes 28 data items – covering membership information, portfolio data, and financial performance – and enables programme management and field staff to identify differences in performance across the groups of each trainer. A focused, periodic analysis of differences in group performance helps to identify problems, allowing programme management to take corrective action promptly and systematically. Ultimately this system improves the safety, operating efficiency, and financial performance of the savings groups being trained. Groups that report an abnormally low return on member investment, for example, may have loan repayment problems or weaknesses in recordkeeping that compromise the accuracy of group records. These groups should be prioritized for supervisory visits, and given remedial training as necessary.

Data requirements

The financial logic of the software is grounded on a balance-sheet approach that captures the membership data, assets, liabilities, and member equity of each group at discrete points in time. This approach also imputes both actual and forecasted measures of financial performance. In other words, the software is not predicated upon the use of a specific recordkeeping system, historical data, or data inputs at fixed intervals. The system is equally suited to institutions that promote memory-based recordkeeping, a passbook-based system, a more formal ledger-based system, or a combination of these methods.

The fundamental principles in the design of the MIS are:

1. group recordkeeping requirements should not be beyond the reach of moderately literate populations;

2. data requirements should be limited to the data generated directly through normal operations and records of savings groups; and
3. the system should not require overly complex or copious data collection activities that burden programme staff or groups.

Depending on the group records and the meeting procedures promoted by the facilitating agency, the required data should largely be observable to programme staff during the normal operations of a group meeting.

The core data requirements of the system include 23 items at the level of each group.[2] Among these items, 20 are either fixed or observable during the normal operations of a group meeting. The three remaining items relate to member savings and outstanding loans, and require an examination of the group's primary records – verbal, passbooks, or ledgers. Experienced field staff can normally collect this data in less than 10 minutes following a normal group meeting. Data is collected and entered into the system at a frequency determined by the project – typically monthly or quarterly.

Outputs

Table 6.1 summarizes the outputs of the MIS (membership data, portfolio data and financial performance, and efficiency of the implementing agency) according to each report and level of analysis – group, field staff or area portfolio, and the overall project. These outputs are automatically generated by the system, and based on no more than the routine data collection outlined above.

The VSL Aggregator Tool enables users to aggregate the data from up to 100 MIS files. The tool has proven to be extremely useful as country programmes are implemented by an increasing number of partner NGOs and local offices, each using a unique MIS installation represented by a unique file.

Data quality and integrity

The most recent version of the MIS includes a data validation tool that is expected to significantly improve data quality and integrity. A series of nine logical constraints prevents the entry of mathematically impossible data, and the total number of data entry errors is indicated on the Overall Project Performance Report. The system also identifies and flags groups with reported financial performance outside a common range, and alerts programme management to atypical results.

User-defined content and customized tools

The VSL MIS allows for a certain degree of customization; users can define up to 17 variables to generate custom indicators. This functionality has become increasingly important as savings groups are promoted by a growing

Table 6.1 Outputs of the VSL MIS, organized by report and level of analysis

Report	Field Officer Portfolio Analysis	Portfolio Performance Comparison	Overall Project Performance	Performance Ratios
Level of analysis	Group	Field officer or area portfolio	Project	Project
Membership data	Group name Group number Linkage to external savings Linkage to external credit Date of first training meeting Date savings started Group trainer Age (no. of weeks) Members at start Registered members at present Percentage change in no. of members Dropout rate Attendance rate Percentage of women	Name of field officer or area No. of field officer or area No. of supervised groups Total no. of registered members Percentage change in no. of members Dropout rate Attendance rate Percentage of women Percentage of members with loans	Total no. of people assisted by the programme Total no. of current members Total no. of men Total no. of women Total no. of supervised groups Total no. of graduated groups No. of members belonging to graduated groups Average age of groups (weeks) Membership growth rate Attendance rate Member retention rate	Attendance rate Retention rate Membership growth rate
Portfolio data and financial performance of groups	No. of loans outstanding Percentage of members with loans Write-offs Cash in loan fund Cash in other funds Value of loans outstanding Property	Percentage of members with loans Average outstanding loan size Loan fund utilization rate Return on savings Return on assets Annualized return on assets	Assets Cash in loan fund Cash in other funds Value of loans outstanding Property Liabilities and member equity Liabilities	Average savings per member Average outstanding loan size Return on savings Return on assets Annualized return on assets Average write-off per graduated group Percentage of members with loans

Report	Field Officer Portfolio Analysis	Portfolio Performance Comparison	Overall Project Performance	Performance Ratios
	Debts		Member equity	Loans outstanding as a percentage of total assets
	Savings		Average member equity	
	Profits/loss		Savings	
	Member equity		Average savings per member	
	Return on savings		Retained earnings (imputed profits)	
			Average profit per member to date	
	Return on assets		No. of loans outstanding	
	Annualized return on assets		Value of loans outstanding	
			Average outstanding loan size	
			Average value of loans outstanding per group	
			Unpaid balance of late loans	
			Portfolio at risk	
			Average write-off per graduated group	
			Write-offs this period	
			Loan fund utilization rate	
			Return on savings	
			Return on assets	
			Annualized return on assets	
Efficiency of implementing agency			Ratio of field officers to total staff	Ratio of field officers to total staff
			Caseload: groups per field officer	Caseload: groups per field officer
			Caseload: registered members per field	Caseload: registered members per field
			Total expenditure to date	Cost per member assisted
			Cost per member assisted	

number and variety of institutions, as well as within a greater variety of multi-sectoral programmes. The MIS enables users to introduce descriptive data and performance metrics that meet their particular monitoring needs, as well as those of their donors. Until recently, projects that required monitoring of any aspects of group performance outside the MIS's standardized configuration were obliged to use parallel tools. The most recent version of the MIS enables users to integrate group performance indicators in any area – literacy, education, food security, poverty levels, financial inclusion, group dynamics, etc. – into a single tool.

Most user-defined content is generated at the level of a project, based on its particular monitoring needs and those of its donors. Recently, however, several implementing agencies have, to varying extents, systematized their user-defined content across their global programming, in an effort to track group performance around a set of indicators that reflect their vision and objectives. Table 6.2 identifies the user-defined variables tracked by various implementing agencies.

In addition to user-defined content, several implementing agencies have developed parallel tools to complement the standard MIS. CARE's MIS Compiler both compiles the data of all groups and assesses the data quality for each individual group based on a series of mathematical constraints. This Excel-based tool automatically generates an error report highlighting groups with implausible data and results outside the normal range. The CARE MIS Compiler also enables users to aggregate data from files of different versions of the MIS and at multiple levels (data can be aggregated at the country, region, and international level, for instance, while the VSL Aggregator Tool is limited to a single level of aggregation).

Catholic Relief Services' (CRS) Savings and Internal Lending Community (SILC) programme has designed its own 'brownie system', which rates the programme performance and quality of data management of each of its 28 country programmes on a quarterly basis. This index is based on the timeliness of reporting, the completeness of data, the completeness of an accompanying analytical report, and three quantitative benchmarks of overall programme performance, which identify variances in performance as well as data quality.

Similarly, the Aga Khan Foundation has developed a process to ensure the quality of MIS data and to identify groups that require additional supervision or immediate attention. On a quarterly basis, all the MIS files of the global programme are audited in order to identify implausible data, weaknesses in data collection, and groups with atypically positive or negative performance. The outcomes of the quarterly data audit are communicated to each country programme through a quarterly progress report, which also includes an analysis of the overall programme performance. Initially, the data audit was conducted through a simple spreadsheet with a series of mathematical constraints, to which the MIS data was exported and analysed. The development of the data

Table 6.2 User-defined variables

Aga Khan Foundation	Catholic Relief Services	CARE	Oxfam
Group survival rate	Village name	Share price	Frequency of meetings
Cumulative outreach of the programme, disaggregated by gender	Cycle of operation	Group monthly interest rate	Meeting day and time
Cumulative outreach of the programme, disaggregated by age[1]	Group payment to community-based trainer for SILC services	No. of women accessing loans	Share-out amount
Meeting attendance rate, disaggregated by gender[1]	Payment arrangement for community-based trainer	Group location	Group contact information
Member retention rate, disaggregated by gender[1]	No. of members participating in business skills training	No. of group members with disabilities	Group location
Percentage of members that have taken a loan during the training cycle	Price for business skills training	GPS coordinates	End date of current cycle of operation
Percentage of members that have received support from the Social Fund during the training cycle	Group payment to community-based trainer for business skills training		
Group location and contact information	Cumulative no. of groups, disaggregated by average age of members (child, youth and adult)[1]		
	No. of self-replicated groups arising from supported groups[1]		

1 optional, country or region-specific user-defined variables

validation tool in the most recent version of the MIS has greatly facilitated and automated this process.

And finally, CRS has also developed an *MIS Analysis Tool* to complement the standard MIS. The tool is based on the Field Officer Portfolio Analysis section of the MIS and contains a series of filters which enables the user to conduct a more nuanced analysis of group performance, as well as the operational efficiency of field staff and community-based trainers.

Limitations in current approaches

The main limitation of the primary performance monitoring tool used by the sector – the VSL Management Information System – is that it is static. A meaningful analysis of group, field staff, area, or project performance requires the analysis of trends, which is not directly possible in the current tool. Historical group data is not stored, but is rather eliminated through the entry of new data. Implementing agencies have circumvented this limitation by storing multiple files and creating parallel spreadsheets and databases to analyse performance trends. The next generation of the VSL MIS will be fully integrated with the Savings Groups Information Exchange[3] (SAVIX), with online and offline capabilities that will allow users to store historical programme data in a single location and access a broader range of database functions unavailable under the current Excel platform.

Secondly, financial results in the current version of the VSL MIS are generated based on a balance-sheet approach; group profits are imputed based on changes in member equity rather than a proper income statement. In other words, the financial logic of the VSL MIS assumes that the group will recover all its assets (primarily its outstanding loans to its members) and repay all its debts to outside individuals or financial institutions before member savings are fully distributed to the membership, along with retained earnings. These assumptions are generally acceptable to practitioners, given the undesirable alternative: the promotion of formal financial statements, including a proper income-statement calculation of profit, that would grossly complicate group recordkeeping and undermine the independence, autonomy, and sustainability of savings groups.

Thirdly, measures of returns on both savings and assets are understated by the current set of tools: the denominator is the current value (of savings or assets) as opposed to the average value over the period. This approach is necessitated by the practical constraint of measuring average savings or assets over the period of analysis; most group recordkeeping systems are unable to easily generate this information, and approximations are difficult because the financial growth of savings groups is not at all linear. On the other hand, the linear annualization of returns generally overestimates the actual returns of savings groups over a one-year period, as time-bound groups that have periodic share-outs generally experience a significant decline in loan activity toward the end of the period. The shorter the operating period, the more significant the difference between annualized returns and actualized returns over a one-year period.

Fourthly, practitioners have recently recognized the importance of inter-cycle dynamics in the performance of savings groups and discussions of sustainability. In time-bound savings groups, the period between the share-out and the next cycle of operations can vary significantly in duration and in rates of re-investment by returning group members to initiate the new cycle. Common developments in the inter-cycle period include the entry and exit of members, splintering of the group into multiple groups, spontaneous replication of new groups around the initial group, and collective economic activity based on the funds generated by the share-out. Current approaches to performance monitoring do not capture this period in the life cycle of savings groups, which some practitioners argue is fundamental to understanding their performance and sustainability.

Management information systems at the frontier: the future of performance monitoring for savings groups

VSL Management Information System: the next generation

The VSL Management Information System is the result of nearly a decade of collaboration in the sector to standardize performance metrics and provide facilitating agencies with a relatively simple, yet effective tool to monitor the performance of savings groups. Its use by several hundreds of projects in all areas of the developing world is indicative of its accessibility and usefulness. However, more mature programmes have had to develop parallel tools to meet all their information needs. The system has a number of limitations described in the previous section, and, from a technological perspective, the Excel-based tool has reached its limits.

As a result, VSL Associates and Software Group,[4] with support from the Bill & Melinda Gates Foundation and The MasterCard Foundation, initiated the development of a new, web-based management information system in 2011; a beta version is expected to be released for user-testing by the end of 2012. The new architecture of the system, based on various stakeholder workshops throughout 2011, is designed to meet the information needs of increasingly large and sophisticated implementing agencies that require more advanced reporting and performance measurement. Above all, the new MIS will be web-based to better integrate with the SAVIX, and to eventually eliminate the costs associated with version upgrades, error fixing, and maintaining a large number of independent MIS installations.

The new MIS will contain database functionalities allowing users to store, filter, analyse, and report data at the required level of analysis; it will also maintain historical data to enable analysis of trends. The web-based system will have online and offline capabilities that enable users to update data in real-time, or to upload their data to a defined network at their discretion. Users will also be able to define and structure networks that will facilitate reporting and analysis at multiple levels, from area teams, to local offices, to projects, to country programmes, grantors, and global programmes. Finally, the new MIS will be designed to allow facilitating agencies to integrate the system with mobile data collection through smartphones.

CARE Mobile Management Information System

In 2010, CARE forged a partnership with ViewWorld[5] to develop a web-based version of the MIS. The *CARE Mobile MIS* aims to improve CARE's ability to monitor the performance of its VSL programming at various levels, including regional and country programmes, implementation channels, trainers, and groups.

First and foremost, the online database will improve communication and reporting, gradually replacing the large number of MIS installations under the Excel-based system. Secondly, enhanced database functionalities will enable users to store historical data, generate performance ratios, and conduct trend analysis at the desired level, from the level of CARE's global VSL programme down to individual groups. Thirdly, the system will incorporate additional features to capture basic village information and critical indicators linked to group performance, such as financial linkages, linkages to other service providers, and social performance. Finally, the database will also allow for the integration of other datasets, in particular CARE's VSLA member impact surveys, which record data of all members upon entry into the programme (baseline) and two years later (endline), covering economic welfare, agricultural holdings and production, housing conditions, education, food security, access to financial services, women's empowerment, and their role in household decision-making. The system will then allow users to monitor and correlate member impact to individual groups, trainers, delivery channels, and country programmes.

The *CARE Mobile MIS* allows users to upload data through three possible channels, including: 1) through paper data collection sheets, entered into the VSL MIS and then synchronized with CARE's online database; 2) through paper data collection sheets then entered directly into CARE's online database; or 3) through an Android phone, using the *CARE Mobile MIS* application, that transmits the data directly to the online database.

The most innovative feature of the *CARE Mobile MIS* is its smartphone application, the first of its kind for savings groups. CARE and ViewWorld have developed this application for the collection of savings group performance data, replacing the paper data collection and transmission methods used today in the Excel-based MIS. 'The majority of data management errors occur at the moment of data collection', explains Sybil Chidiac, Senior Technical Adviser of CARE's Access Africa initiative. 'Under the mobile data collection method, data validation occurs at the moment of collection. The system alerts the field staff to questionable data and prevents the user from moving forward when impossible data is entered. This will minimize the frequency of errors and greatly improve data quality.'

The smartphone application also automatically records the GPS coordinates of the group, resulting in a map of programme coverage generated by the *CARE Mobile MIS*. Each group is represented by a point on the map, including four key performance indicators of the group. CARE's Access Africa initiative recognizes three main uses of programme mapping:

1. *Understanding financial inclusion.* Groups have existed for so long off the radar; knowing where these groups are located and their access to financial services is a stepping stone to financial inclusion.
2. *Promotion of financial linkages.* Cross-referencing the location and socio-demographic data of groups with branches and agents of commercial banks, MFIs, and mobile money agents informs the conversation with financial institutions, identifying the specific needs of groups and their locations.

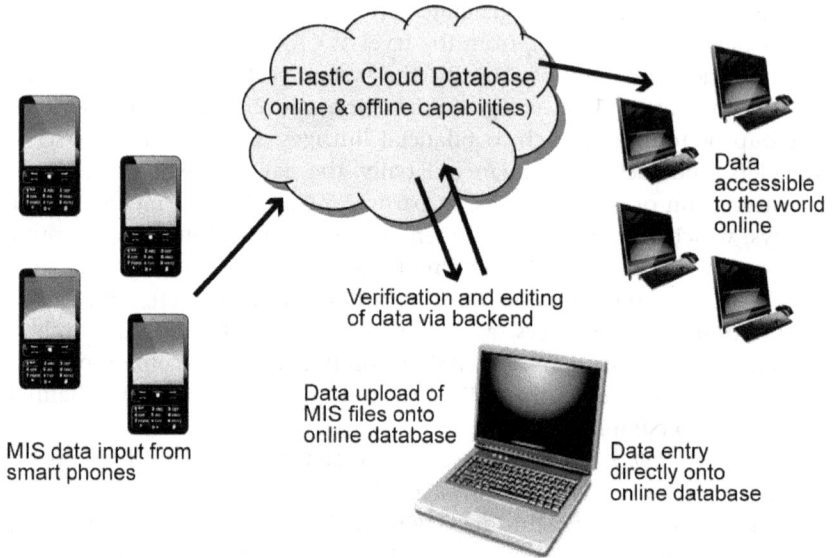

Figure 6.1 CARE Mobile Management Information System

3. *Advocacy and the promotion of complementary services.* Identifying a critical mass of groups in a specific area with a common need facilitates a response.

The online database comprises a hosted database system, which secures all data in the cloud. Data can be accessed either through a web interface, or through a smartphone as illustrated in Figure 6.1.

Any registered user will be able to access the database through CARE's Access Africa website, currently in development. Furthermore, as data is transmitted directly to the online database, the system will provide trainers with an immediate analysis of group performance. Any resulting issues identified by the MIS may be addressed at once by the trainer, rather than awaiting the periodic analysis of programme data or a visit by programme management.

The ViewWorld system is based on open source technology, and the back-end systems as well as the mobile applications are released under an open source licence. The *CARE Mobile MIS* and smartphone application are currently under user-testing, and CARE expects that the technologies will be available from ViewWorld by the end of 2012.

Oxfam America: programme mapping and spatial analysis

'The full value of programme mapping is not fully understood until it is actually completed', explains Janina Matuszeski, Research Coordinator in the Community Finance Department at Oxfam America. 'Mapping and data visualization is a useful tool, but it is an abstract idea and its exact uses cannot be determined until results are generated.' In Mali, Oxfam America mapped the evolution of its Saving for Change programme (SfC) from 2005 to 2010. Under the initiative, *Visualizing SfC*, Oxfam America generated two time-series mapping tools:

1. *Programme coverage*: This type of map illustrates the cumulative number of groups in each commune of the programme area and in each year from 2005 to 2010; it also correlates programme outreach to regional poverty rates. The map shows the depth of outreach both across the area of operation and over time.
2. *Savings mobilization*: This type of map illustrates the average savings balance of groups in each commune of the programme area, in each year from 2005 to 2010. This map also shows the savings mobilization performance of the programme over the working area and over time. Figure 6.2 is an example of the savings mobilization map for one programme partner of SfC in Mali.

Oxfam America is planning to introduce the *Visualizing SfC* initiative in Cambodia and Senegal. 'Programme mapping is a relatively new activity at Oxfam America, and is a powerful tool for internal communication and

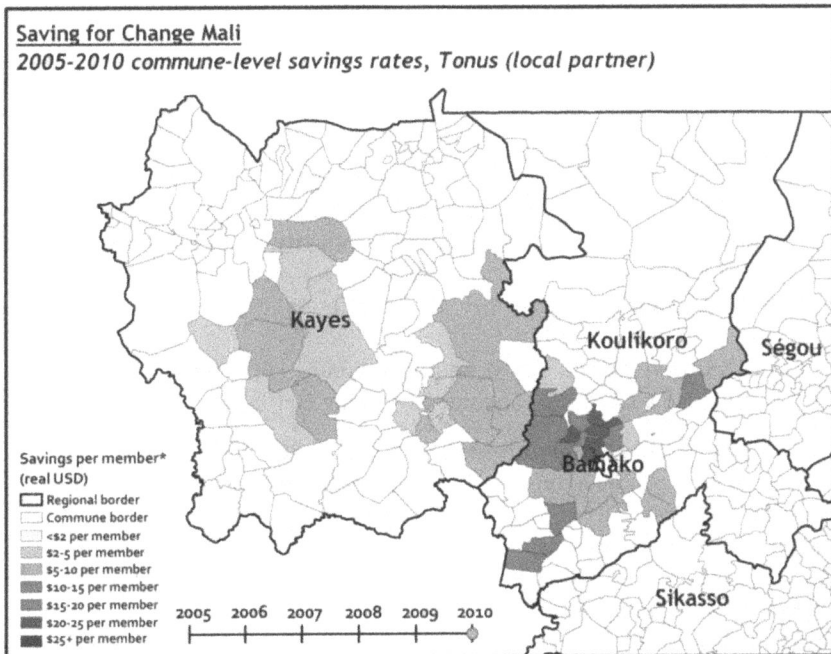

Figure 6.2 Saving for Change programme map, Tonus (local partner), Mali
Source: Lynnae Ruberg, Oxfam America

fundraising', says Matuszeski. 'It may become extremely useful in programme planning, and in understanding the overlap and potential integration of savings groups with other Oxfam programmes.'

Freedom from Hunger: Social Indicator System

Freedom from Hunger (FFH) uses the VSL Management Information System to monitor the performance of field staff and savings groups in its global Saving for Change programme. While the MIS measures primarily the financial performance of savings groups, it does not measure social performance, such as changes in the social capital or food security of savings group members. In order to fill this gap, Freedom from Hunger is developing a *Social Indicator System*.

The purpose of the *FFH Social Indicator System* (FFH SIS) is to measure how members' attitudes, knowledge, and general living conditions change during their participation in Saving for Change. The SIS uses an Excel-based spreadsheet to record member baseline and endline data; it can also be used as an ongoing monitoring system. The FFH SIS includes five sections:

1. *Respondent Demographics*: Basic group and member data including group name, location, and age, as well as member name, age, gender, and duration of programme participation.
2. *Social Capital and Empowerment*: Indicators of social capital and member confidence.
3. *Indicators on Relevant Education Topics*: Indicators of knowledge retention and behavioural change, customized to the educational curriculum of the implementing agency.
4. *Progress Out of Poverty Index*: 'The Progress out of Poverty Index™ (PPI) is a simple and accurate tool that measures poverty levels of groups and individuals [...] and tracks changes in poverty levels over time [...] The PPI is a composite of 10 easy-to-collect, country-specific, non-financial indicators such as family size, the number of children attending school and the type of housing.'[6]
5. *Food Security Survey*: Based on the standard FFH Food Security Survey with some adaptation for country-specific factors.

In order to keep the implementation of the FFH SIS low-cost and manageable by partners, the baseline and endline surveys are undertaken by field staff with one or two randomly-selected members of each of the groups for which they are responsible. Each survey takes 30 to 40 minutes, and is administered during a regular group visit. Survey data is entered into the system manually, and the SIS automatically generates a report accompanied by an analysis of the results. The report enables programme management to identify differences in performance across programme areas and field staff, and to resolve weaknesses. For example, if survey results on malaria education indicate that group members trained by a particular staff member do not know that only mosquitoes cause malaria, then that staff member may need additional training. The FFH SIS will be finalized and field-tested by FFH partner institutions in 2012; FFH aims to then introduce the system as part of its technical assistance package to Saving for Change partner institutions.

The Savings Groups Information Exchange

The Savings Groups Information Exchange (www.thesavix.org) is an online reporting system that provides transparent, standardized data on savings groups. The SAVIX collects and validates financial and operational data from over 80,000 savings groups in all regions of the developing world, as well as from the agencies that promote them. As of the second quarter 2012, 142 projects in 22 countries were reporting to the SAVIX on a voluntary basis, uploading quarterly programme data to the site through a data exportation tool embedded in the VSL Management Information System.

Benchmarking and informed decision-making are critical to achieving high-quality programme results. The aim of the site is to facilitate analysis, develop norms, and improve performance sector-wide.

The SAVIX also invites all projects and implementing agencies to have their data rated. Using a standard data accuracy measurement tool, the SAVIX gives projects one to four stars based on the accuracy of their primary records at the level of the group and field staff. Data ratings provide practitioners, donors, and industry observers an objective evaluation of the completeness and accuracy of projects' self-reported data.

Qualitative monitoring

The management and geographic information systems presented in the previous sections focus on the financial performance of savings groups, and on the efficiency of the agencies that promote them. Practitioners have also developed a series of qualitative tools and processes to assess the quality of savings groups under their training and supervision. Implementing agencies employ diverse qualitative tools and approaches, but assessments of group quality invariably revolve around the following themes: understanding and adherence to the methodology promoted by the implementing agency, good governance, operational capacity of the group and its members, accuracy and clarity of group records, participative decision-making, safety of group funds – and, above all, transparency, including members' understanding of their own financial position and that of the group.

VSL Associates has developed two qualitative tools to assess the quality of savings groups. The VSLA Health Diagnosis and Change of Phase Form is used by field staff and their supervisors to assess the capacity of groups and their ability to move to the next stage on the training schedule, characterized by less frequent visits from the trainer. The assessment comprises 15 items that are observable during a normal meeting and do not require any additional inquiries. In 2011, the VSLA Health Diagnosis and Change of Phase Form was digitized and renamed the Consolidated VSLA Evaluation Tool. The new tool allows implementing agencies to customize assessment criteria and weight each criterion. The Excel-based tool generates an automatic assessment of each group, the overall group quality across the project, the variance in group quality across evaluated groups, and the relative strengths and weaknesses of the project with respect to the 15 assessment criteria.

The Consolidated VSLA Evaluation Tool has been adopted by numerous implementing agencies and is now an integral component of all project assessments of the Aga Khan Foundation and Plan International. Catholic Relief Services has customized the original VSLA Health Diagnosis and Change of Phase Form, and developed its own Group-Agent Assessment Template. Performed by supervisors, the assessment examines 30 items related to meeting procedures, group functioning, and the behaviour and effectiveness of the trainer. The assessment also includes an analysis of the quality of group records and information generated by the group and the trainer.

Similarly, the SfC Consortium – composed of Freedom from Hunger, Oxfam America, and the Stromme Foundation – has developed its own tool to assess the quality of groups in its Saving for Change programme. The unique feature of the SfC Group Assessment Tool is its simplicity: the assessment is based on eight simple criteria, with the objective that community-based trainers become enabled to conduct it. And finally, CARE's Access Africa Questionnaire to Assess Group Quality is a more comprehensive tool that assesses group quality and the alignment of group and project activities with the principles of CARE's VSLA programme. The questionnaire employs mixed research methods including the observation of meeting procedures, the examination of group and member records, and focus group discussions. It includes reminders to the group, trainer, and project managers about the fundamental principles of the programme and recommended best practices. At present, the tool is employed by Access Africa in the assessment of its country programmes, but the objective is to systematize its use in routine monitoring and eventually extend it to CARE's partner institutions.

Long-term monitoring

The rapid growth in the outreach of savings groups has attracted increasing levels of interest in their long-term performance. Through increasingly rigorous monitoring and evaluation systems, facilitating agencies are making greater efforts to better understand the performance, dynamics, and survival rate of independent groups beyond the training period. For example, in 2010 the Aga Khan Foundation's Community-based Savings programme adopted a global monitoring, evaluation, and learning plan, under which a statistically-significant random sample of independent groups will be tracked for two to four years in all its country programmes worldwide. The *Aga Khan Foundation MEL Plan* aims to broaden the perspective on the outcomes of savings groups,

Table 6.3 SAVIX research sample results

Indicator	2010	2011
Cumulative no. of members	7,261	7,621
Cumulative no. of groups	332	326
Total assets (US$)	182,589	251,933
Average no. of members per group	21.9	23.4
Attendance rate (%)	86	83
Retention rate (%)	99	99
Average outstanding loan size (US$)	36.31	43.05
Women members (%)	77	79
Savings as percentage of loans outstanding (%)	106	103
Savings per member as percentage of GNI per capita	4.3	5.9
Average outstanding loan size as percentage of GNI per capita	6.8	8.1
Percentage of members with loans outstanding	53	60
Loans outstanding as a percentage of performing assets	81	80
Annualized return on assets	47.8	49.1
Annualized return on equity	48.3	45.4
Group survival rate	100	98.2

tracking their performance over an extended period of time and providing more rigorous estimates of group survival rates.

Nevertheless, it remains a serious challenge for practitioners to monitor the long-term performance of savings groups once they leave an area, or beyond a project's lifespan. The few studies on the long-term performance of savings groups are very narrow in scope, limited to end-of-project evaluations and specific projects and institutions.

The SAVIX – with support from the Bill & Melinda Gates Foundation, Catholic Relief Services, CARE, Oxfam America, and VSL Associates – launched a five-year panel study in 2009 to describe the performance of a random sample of 332 savings groups, which were mobilized and trained by 33 projects in six countries. In the first quarter of each year, standardized data is collected from all active groups in the sample, and the results are consolidated and published on the SAVIX. The results from 2010 and 2011 – roughly 6 and 18 months after group formation, respectively – are displayed in Table 6.3.

Conclusion

Since the external evaluator stepped into that dusty storage room nearly a decade ago and was buried under mounds of endless surveys and group records, the community-based microfinance sector has matured tremendously in its monitoring tools and approaches. In 2004, the Savings-Led Financial Services Working Group of the SEEP Network initiated the dialogue on standardized reporting in community-based microfinance, culminating in the 2008 paper 'Ratio Analysis of Community-Managed Microfinance Programs'.

Building upon the increased information management needs of the sector and its growing commitment to standardized reporting, VSL Associates developed the sector's first management information system in 2006, which has undergone numerous iterations and is now used by hundreds of projects all over developing world.

The increasing sophistication of the sector in recent years has also accelerated the pace of innovation in monitoring savings groups, resulting in some particularly promising initiatives. The latest version of the VSL Management Information System is a powerful yet simple, accessible, and cost-effective tool for experienced practitioners as well as new entrants into the sector. Both VSL Associates and CARE's Access Africa programme are developing more sophisticated, web-based databases and mobile data transmission tools for larger programmes, implemented by a growing number of local institutions in more remote areas. Oxfam America and CARE are also delving into programme mapping, spatial analysis, and geographic information systems, changing the way we understand and communicate the outreach, performance, and needs of savings groups. Freedom from Hunger is challenging the sector to consider the social performance of savings groups, integrating member impact surveys into its routine monitoring and Social Indicator System. The SAVIX now provides practitioners with the largest (and rapidly expanding) dataset on savings groups; it also includes powerful tools of analysis and benchmarking to support informed decision-making, development of norms, and improved performance of the overall sector. Finally, nearly all of the major international NGOs that promote savings groups have adopted, customized, and refined qualitative tools to assess the quality of savings groups under their supervision.

As the sector continues to develop its information management practices and tools, implementation agencies will have to balance the needs of various stakeholders in the performance monitoring of savings groups. These stakeholders include donors, programme management, and groups themselves. Above all, the value of any monitoring tools and practices must be measured against the usefulness of the actionable information they generate for their stakeholders, as well as the costs – financial and non-financial – of developing and maintaining the system.

Acknowledgements

The author is grateful for the contributions and comments received from Guy Vanmeenen, marc bavois, Kathy Younker, Candace Nelson, Laura Fleischer Proaño, Megan Gash, Hugh Allen, Jeffrey Ashe, Andrea Teebagy, Janina Matuszeski, Sophie Romana, Sybil Chidiac, and Abdoul Karim Coulibaly. Any errors or omissions remain his own.

Notes

1. The SEEP Network Savings-Led Financial Services Working Group: Ratios Sub-Group. *Ratio Analysis of Community-Managed Microfinance Programs.* SEEP Network, 2008.
2. In addition to these core data requirements, project-level staffing and expenditure information is needed to generate indicators of the project's operational and financial efficiency.
3. The Savings Groups Information Exchange (www.thesavix.org) is an online reporting system that provides transparent and standardized data on savings groups. The SAVIX collects and validates financial and operational data from over 80,000 savings groups in all regions of the developing world, and on the agencies that promote them.
4. Software Group is a microfinance service provider committed to the use of appropriate and affordable technology within the sector (www.softwaregroup-bg.com).
5. ViewWorld is a private company with an explicit social profile, The company provides speedy, credible, and efficient communication and reporting tools to humanitarian organizations in Africa (www.viewworld.dk).
6. Progress out of Poverty is an initiative of the Grameen Foundation and the Consultative Group to Assist the Poorest (CGAP). The Progress out of Poverty index (PPI) is based on an approach developed by Mark Shreiner of Microfinance Risk Management, LLC and, to date, the Grameen Foundation has commissioned national PPI indices in over 40 countries <http://progressoutofpoverty.org>.

About the author

David Panetta is Technical Adviser to the Community-based Savings programme of the Aga Khan Foundation. Through the promotion of savings groups, AKF provides access to basic, appropriate, and sustainable financial services in some of the most marginalized areas of Afghanistan, India, Madagascar, Mozambique, Pakistan, Tajikistan, and Tanzania. Previously, David worked with VSL Associates and supported community-based microfinance programmes in over 20 countries in Africa, Asia and Latin America, providing support in programme design, training, performance monitoring, programme evaluation, and research. David lived in Bangladesh from 2004 to 2008, where he studied with Grameen Bank, served as a research fellow with the Palli-Karma Sahayak Foundation (the national microfinance apex fund), and worked as Microfinance Programme Manager at the Chars Livelihoods Programme of DFID.

Index

About The SEEP Network

The SEEP Network is a global network of over 130 international practitioner organizations dedicated to combating poverty through promoting inclusive markets and financial systems. SEEP represents the largest and most diverse network of its kind, comprising international development organizations and global, regional, and country-level practitioner networks that promote market development and financial inclusion. Members are active in 170 countries and support nearly 90 million entrepreneurs and their families.

This book was produced in partnership with The MasterCard Foundation. The views expressed in this book should not be seen as necessarily reflecting those of The MasterCard Foundation or its employees.

About The MasterCard Foundation

The MasterCard Foundation advances microfinance and youth learning to promote financial inclusion and prosperity. Through collaboration with committed partners in over 48 developing countries, it is helping people living in poverty to access opportunities to learn and prosper. Based in Toronto, Canada, the Foundation was established through the generosity of MasterCard Worldwide at the time of the company's initial public offering in 2006. It operates independently of MasterCard Worldwide. For more information, visit http://mastercardfdn.org.

www.ingramcontent.com/pod-product-compliance
Lightning Source LLC
Chambersburg PA
CBHW072135020426
42334CB00018B/1811